"If you are expecting *Unshakable Faith* to be a well written, accurate and factual account of African American history, you will not be disappointed. The depth of faith and the inspiration of the Spirit of God is revealed in unmistakable fashion throughout every page. I was elated and surprised to read such compelling truths of real-life experiences. If you have ever asked the question, 'How did African Americans survive and thrive in four hundred years of oppression?' Dr. Latimore has your answer."

—**Rev. Dr. Otis I. Mitchell**, pastor, Mount Zion First Baptist Church, San Antonio, Texas

"It is not common to see the 'unshakable faith' of deep Christian discipleship joined with a deep passion for the realized unity of Christ's church. Carey Latimore has lived a life-changing commitment to both, and this book reveals how and why his vision must be lived afresh. By choosing to reveal these stories, he shows us how our long-standing racial divides can be healed by true stories of faith and courage. Here you will learn from great Christians, most of whom you never knew. You will also see the priority of healing the plague of our disunity that is rooted in racial stereotypes and profound mistrust."

– **John H. Armstrong**, founder, The Initiative; author, *Tear Down These Walls: Following Jesus into Deeper Unity*

"Carey Latimore's *Unshakable Faith* is a powerful combination of hope, history, and storytelling where he takes us on a historical journey told through the lives of African Americans and our country—reminding us that while we cannot erase the pain and sorrow of our imperfect lives, we can choose to live in joy driven by an unshakable faith."

> —**Juan Sepúlveda, J.D.**, Visiting Radford Professor of Practice in Urban Education, Trinity University

"Dr. Latimore has written a devotional history of African Americans that is as well grounded in historical scholarship as it is spiritually challenging for believers, especially African American Christians. This work will do much to grow believers into mature Christlikeness. Dr. Latimore has done a great service to the Church."

> —**H. Paul Thompson Jr., PhD**, author, *A Most Stirring and Significant Episode: Religion and the Rise and Fall of Prohibition in Black Atlanta, 1865–1887*

"*Unshakable Faith* is a spiritual and scholarly examination of the importance of the Christian faith in the African American community. Drawing from a variety of sources, Latimore deftly explores the ways individuals as diverse as Phillis Wheatley and Thomas A. Dorsey relied on unshakable faith not only to survive but to thrive. In difficult times such as those we currently live in, Latimore's book is prayerful, insightful, and hope-inspiring."

> —**Lawrence Scott, PhD**, executive director, Community for Life Foundation; assistant professor, Texas A&M University–San Antonio

"*Unshakable Faith* by Dr. Carey Latimore is one of those rare books that inspires, motivates, and empowers the reader. . . . Dr. Latimore provides historical context for the many brilliant African American men and women, past and present, whose faith and dedication to God provided the foundation for them to persevere regardless of the harsh mental and physical reality in which they lived."

—**Angelica Docog**, executive director, Polish Center, Panna Maria, Texas

"With eloquence and simplicity, Dr. Latimore presents a moving account of both historical and current figures—and candidly shares part of his own history—illuminating the past and the present, and challenging us not only to have unshakable faith but to live it."

—**Geraldine Guadagno**, author, *Blessed Chiara Badano: Her Secrets to Happiness*

UNSHAKABLE FAITH

African American Stories of
Redemption, Hope, and Community

Carey H. Latimore IV

Our Daily Bread
Publishing™

Requests for permission to quote from this book should be directed to: Permissions Department, Our Daily Bread Publishing, PO Box 3566, Grand Rapids, MI 49501, or contact us by email at permissionsdept@odb.org.

Scripture quotations, unless otherwise indicated, are taken from the Holy Bible, New International Version®, NIV®. Copyright © 1973, 1978, 1984, 2011 by Biblica, Inc.™ Used by permission of Zondervan. All rights reserved worldwide. www.zondervan.com.

Scripture quotations marked ESV are taken from the ESV® Bible (The Holy Bible, English Standard Version®), copyright © 2001 by Crossway, a publishing ministry of Good News Publishers. Used by permission. All rights reserved.

Interior design by Faceout Studio

Library of Congress Cataloging-in-Publication Data
Names: Latimore, Carey H., author.
Title: Unshakable faith : African American stories of redemption, hope, and
   community / Carey H. Latimore, IV.
Description: Grand Rapids, MI : Our Daily Bread Publishing, [2021] |
   Includes bibliographical references. | Summary: "Be challenged by
   stories of African Americans who reveal a Christianity that offers hope,
   community, and even forgiveness"-- Provided by publisher.
Identifiers: LCCN 2021034612 | ISBN 9781640701069
Subjects: LCSH: African Americans--Religion. | African American
   Christians--Biography. | BISAC: RELIGION / Christian Living / Social
   Issues | RELIGION / Christian Living / Inspirational
Classification: LCC BR563.B53 L38 2021 | DDC 200.89/96073--dc23
LC record available at https://lccn.loc.gov/2021034612

Printed in the United States of America
22 23 24 25 26 27 28 29 / 8 7 6 5 4 3 2 1

This book is dedicated to my mother, Ann Stephens Latimore. Born with sickle cell anemia, my mother also grew up in the underbelly of the Jim Crow South. Surviving illness and segregation, she boldly proclaimed the gospel of Jesus Christ her entire life. When doctors initially gave her fewer than eighteen years to live, she relied on the faith she first learned of through her parents. Not only did she live well beyond the doctors' prognoses, but she also worked as an educator for more than thirty years in three states. This project, along with its potential impact, was one of the last discussions I had with her in person before her condition declined to the point that she was unable to speak to me. She was excited about the potential of this book to encourage people to hold fast to their faith during difficult times. She died in August 2018 at seventy-nine years of age. It is with tremendous gratitude and appreciation that I dedicate this to the woman who introduced me to the power of prayer.

Thank you, Mama, for everything. I will always love you.

CONTENTS

Chapter 1: Finding Freedom in Christ

The lives of Phillis Wheatley and Cyrus Bustill demonstrate the power of faith to sustain, to enable forgiveness, to inspire, and to help build the kingdom of God. The United States of America's motto is *e pluribus unum*, which means "from many come one." During the colonial period, Black people came from various nations only to encounter a new and diverse world.

Chapter 2: Sons and Daughters of the American Revolution

Lott Cary's and Maria Stewart's stories reveal how Black people turned inward and relied on their faith to focus on building strong families, communities, and organizations as an expression of their love of God and their nation. While the American Revolution and Christianity provided them a map for community development, African Americans quickly recognized that the promises and principles written into the Declaration of Independence and the Constitution did not automatically extend to them.

Chapter 3: Journey to Canaan: Freedom and Independence

Harriet Tubman and Booker T. Washington used their prophetic voices to combat slavery and the horrors of racism.

Black people relied on their faith to make the journey from slavery to freedom symbolic of the sojourn of the Israelites in Canaan.

Thomas A. Dorsey, Ethel Waters, and Duke Ellington expressed assurance in their redemption and helped others find freedom. Music was a primary vehicle for Black people to express their belief in redemption. Whether gospel, blues, spirituals, or jazz, Black music has always reflected the people's voices.

The legacies of Mary McLeod Bethune and Fannie Lou Hamer encourage all to see that the cause to eradicate American hatred and oppression is in line with our Christian principles. Even though the struggle for justice has never been easy, our faith informs us that God has not given us a spirit of fear (2 Timothy 1:7).

Kendrick Lamar, Chance the Rapper, and Kanye West reflect new spiritual journeys and experiences that connect them to the past struggles of African American Christians.

FOREWORD

I have devoted the last fifty years of my life to two great passions. The first is the study of the Bible, both as a source of personal, spiritual formation and as the basis of my preaching ministry as a pastor of thirty-four years and a seminary professor for just as long. The second is the study of African American history, with a special focus on the little-known facts about the men and women whose contributions have been most widely associated with this historical narrative. I have developed a set of classroom syllabi and a library of technical resources, both of which reflect my two lifelong passions.

It had never occurred to me until I read this book by Carey Latimore that my two great interests could be addressed at the same time. I had always approached the study of Scripture and the study of African American history as separate scholarly studies, separate academic courses, separate reading lists, and separate sets of training and expertise. All of that changed as I began to work my way through this book. This book is at the same time inspirational and instructive. It speaks to the power of Scripture and faith to sustain people through the most challenging of circumstances. Then it points to individual persons in the long sweep of African American history who were able to demonstrate what Latimore calls *unshakable faith*.

The first thing to note about this book is its historical scope. It begins with persons who, as Latimore observes, "reached out to the Lord in tough times and at crossroads." That is the basis of the book's title, people who showed unshakable faith during the most trying circumstances life could present. It traces that unshakable faith from the Revolutionary War era in American history by considering such persons as the poetess Phillis Wheatley and Cyrus Bustill, who was instrumental in the formation of the Free African Society in Philadelphia, Pennsylvania, in 1787. We also hear about men like Lott Cary and Paul Cuffee, who looked upon the plight of African Americans in the United States of America and concluded that emigration back to Africa was the best course of action.

This book introduces us to incendiary prophets of freedom ranging from Nat Turner to David Walker. There is Harriet Tubman, who led people out of slavery, and Booker T. Washington, who was born a slave but ended up becoming the founder of Tuskegee Institute (now University) during the height of the Jim Crow era in Alabama. Their faith and spiritual resilience were instrumental in their ability to persevere. The same was true, to varying degrees, for W. E. B. Du Bois and Ida B. Wells-Barnett, who were at work during the days when lynch mob justice was a frequent practice used to terrorize African Americans.

What is especially interesting in Latimore's study is his inclusion of various persons from the world of music and entertainment. He begins with a former blues musician called Georgia Tom whose real name is Thomas A. Dorsey, who would become the great composer of gospel music, including the world-famous hymn "Precious Lord, Take My Hand." He then moves to the singer Ethel Waters, who began as a blues and jazz singer but ended up being a regular singer at crusades led by Billy Graham. Latimore also reminds us that the great Duke Ellington spent much of his final years composing three sacred music concerts. One of my own favorite songs is Mahalia Jackson singing "Come Sunday," which was composed by Duke Ellington. Latimore then considers the lives of contemporary artists Kendrick Lamar, Chance the Rapper, and Kanye West. Not everyone sees these final three musicians in the same light as Latimore does. However, what Latimore is after is not consensus but the personal story and testimony of people who say they have persevered because of their own unshakable faith.

Finally, Latimore reminds us that much of African American history was written by courageous women like Mary McLeod Bethune and Fannie Lou Hamer, who endured much in pursuit of their goals of education for Bethune and voting rights for Hamer. Most crucial for me, however, is the way he introduces someone of whom I had no previous knowledge, Maria Stewart. Though she was not born into slavery, she was limited to a life of domestic service that was slave-like in its conditions, and she was inspired by David Walker, William Lloyd Garrison, and other antislavery activists.

It was in that role that she gave a speech in Boston in 1833 that seems to be a perfect blending of biblical faith and African American history. Sounding like the language of James 2:20, "Faith without works is dead," Stewart addressed an antislavery audience by saying, "Talk without effort is nothing; you are abundantly capable, gentlemen, of making yourselves men of distinction; and this gross neglect on your part causes my blood to boil. . . . Here is the grand cause which hinders the rise and progress of the people of color. It is their want of laudable ambition and requisite courage." In the view of Maria Stewart, freedom comes only to those who possess *unshakable faith* that allows them to keep the faith under the most trying of circumstances. Meeting Maria Stewart for the first time made reading this entire book a great joy!

I am certain that everyone who reads this book will learn something they never knew before. That is what makes reading such an important enterprise. This book will not disappoint, as it blends biblical faith and historical narrative in a way I had never imagined, but now greatly appreciate.

—Marvin A. McMickle, PhD
president (retired)
Colgate Rochester Crozer Divinity School
Rochester, New York

TO THE READER

For the word of God is alive and active. Sharper than any double-edged sword, it penetrates even to dividing soul and spirit, joints and marrow; it judges the thoughts and attitudes of the heart.

HEBREWS 4:12

My wife and I are blessed to have jobs where we can work from home. Adapting to the realities brought on by the COVID-19 pandemic has been tough on everyone. As an educator, I struggled to adapt to teaching online. Sometimes the virtual connection is perfect, sometimes less so. I've been unable to visit my church in person. I was also unable to visit my father in Virginia until only recently and kept from seeing my wife's family in the Philippines.

I can understand arguments saying that the pandemic has contributed to the number of people suffering from depression, addiction, and anxiety. As humans, we need each other. This outbreak has only added to our sense of isolation.

Nevertheless, as much as we believe that our world has changed with COVID-19—and continuing instances of the wicked legacy of racism—the foundations of life remain the same. In Jesus, we find joy and peace as we open ourselves to a personal relationship with Him. When we also open up our hearts to others, we can still find satisfaction.

As Christians, our testimony—the way we speak about how we came to know Christ and His impact on our lives—inspires others. Throughout history, so many millions have had spiritual journeys that demonstrate how God's children (young, old, and everyone in between) can find peace by reaching out to the Lord. In our quest to make sense of life, we can have joy in tough places. As a Christian, I am excited to see how people from the past have reached out to the Lord in tough times and at crossroads. As a historian who focuses on African American history, I find joy in these stories from the past, stories of unshakable faith.

While I have witnessed progress personally, I have also witnessed dreams deferred.

Our nation's quest to be a better version of ourselves is tough work, particularly as we consider our history. America is long overdue to have a conversation about our past. Some of that is happening right now. But we need more Christian voices at the table. The Word of God can help us navigate these rough waters. Faith can help us come to terms with our past. My ancestors could not run from their history. They had to remember it. I wonder how they could live, knowing that they had been slaves. And how could they live with the fact that the people who owned them also were among their ancestors? Such realities could have destroyed them.

They lived tough lives, and they certainly understood the meaning of unshakable faith. My ancestors' road was not easy. But their journeys taught them the power of embracing life right in front of them. Today tough times stare us in the face, and unshakable faith is needed to help us weather racial tension, pandemics, and other challenges. As in difficult times in the past, we can still rely on Jesus to strengthen us and lead us to the place where peace surpasses our understanding.

It is my hope that these stories of perseverance through unshakable faith will inspire and encourage you in your life's journey.

CHAPTER 1

FINDING FREEDOM IN CHRIST

No longer as a slave, but better than
a slave, as a dear brother. He is very dear to
me but even dearer to you, both as a
fellow man and as a brother in the Lord.

PHILEMON 1:16

In his letter to Philemon, the apostle Paul explored the ways God can transform relationships between different people when we open ourselves to His guidance. At the time Paul wrote his letter to Philemon, Roman law dictated that Philemon's slave Onesimus had few legal rights. If the reader digs just a little deeper into the historical context of this short letter, they will learn more.

Paul was in prison and therefore no longer a free man. Paul's imprisonment certainly made him feel compassion for a slave who had escaped from his master. Perhaps Paul looked at his chains in his jail cell, harboring desires of escaping from his prison just as Onesimus had escaped from his master. Although imprisoned, as a Roman citizen Paul still had more rights than the escaped Onesimus. Even though he had more rights, Paul did not adhere to the social norms of the period. He worked with Onesimus and helped direct him to the Lord.

It is likely that their time together included the Scriptures and prayer. Their relationship not only brought Onesimus to the faith but also could have enhanced Paul's faith and perhaps encouraged him to reject the class distinctions in his society even more. In his letter to the Colossians, probably written during the same period, Paul wrote, "There is no Gentile or Jew, circumcised or uncircumcised, . . . slave or free, but Christ is all, and is in all (Colossians 3:11). One is left to ponder the impact this time with Onesimus had on Paul's interpretation of equality for all in Christ.

Paul's writings explore the mystery that a person can be physically enslaved but spiritually liberated. The opposite is also true. We can be successful in a worldly sense but spiritually and emotionally disenfranchised. For Paul, finding freedom in Christ was the key to happiness and contentment.

Christ has always meant more than race, money, class, or status. Paul demonstrated this ideal by how he treated Onesimus. He saw Onesimus not as a slave but looked beyond this worldly designation to see his humanity. We recognize that Paul's treatment of Onesimus as an equal helped lead him to Christ. It is clear by the way he spoke about him that Paul considered Onesimus someone very special. Paul's words prove that his faith had freed him from viewing people through socioeconomic prejudice, a transition that enlightened him to become a brother to the disenfranchised.

Although Paul never fully challenged the legal validity of first-century slavery in his writings, he did ask Philemon to take a major step toward Onesimus's redemption. Paul had known Philemon, Onesimus's master, for some time. Philemon was a believer, a person of means whose household included slaves. Understanding the power dynamics in the master and slave relationship, what Paul asked of Philemon is stunning. In his letter to Philemon, Paul made the remarkable request that Philemon tear down the barriers between him and his slave. Paul's letter crescendos to his request of Philemon to see his slave "no longer as a slave, but better than a slave, as a dear brother" (1:16).

Paul's faith reveals the ways that God wants to mold His people into one body. In Philemon, we see God working with three different people, calling each of them into a higher state of community. The prisoner, the slave, and the slave master— divided by circumstance but unified by faith. What a model for us today. According to church tradition, each man accepted this grand commission. The apostle Paul became the most prolific apostle of the Christian gospel. According to church tradition, Philemon became a church leader who died a martyr during the reign of the emperor Diocletian. Before dying for his faith, tradition also suggests that Philemon manumitted his new "brother," Onesimus, who later became the bishop of the Church at Ephesus.

Nations and Brotherhoods

E pluribus unum, America's national motto, means "from many come one." Since its dawn, America[1] has been a diverse nation. Bringing its different parts together, however, has always challenged us. Does unity require complete assimilation? True unity should not mean that individuals and groups completely assimilate. Rather, out of all of our differences, we build something new.

From the colonial through early national periods (from 1607 to 1828), Europeans came to what would become the American continent from many different regions and nations.[2] Moreover, people came for different reasons. Groups like the Pilgrims and Puritans wanted to freely practice their Christian faith. Arriving in 1620, the settlers at Plymouth Rock established a separate colony free from the reach of the Anglican Church. Ten years later, the Puritans founded Massachusetts Bay Colony in their desire to purify the Anglican Church. John Winthrop, an early leader of the group, stated that they wanted to establish a community for God—"a City on a Hill." Quoting Jesus's words in Matthew 5:14, Winthrop envisioned a community that people would not only look up to but a gathering of people who would also set a moral standard for the world.[3]

Other peoples established colonies in America to escape religious prejudice, persecution, or exile. In Maryland, Cecil Calvert, a devout Catholic who endured persecution for his faith, became the first proprietor of Maryland colony, establishing it as a place of sanctuary for Christian minorities seeking refuge. In 1649, the colony's assembly passed the Maryland Toleration Act, a law promising religious freedom for all Trinitarian Christians. To the north of Maryland in Rhode Island, Roger Williams, a Puritan who later founded the first Baptist church in America, founded the colony after being forced out of Massachusetts Bay because of his radical religious beliefs (at least in the eyes of the Christian leaders of Massachusetts Bay). Williams eventually established a colony respectful of the principles of faith, fairness, religious freedom, and equality.

Black people had already arrived at the shores of Jamestown even before European colonists arrived at Maryland, Massachusetts Bay, or Rhode Island. Their arrival was not of their choosing. African captives came to America from disparate nations along the coasts of West Africa. Those nations had different languages, different religions, and different ways of life. Little is known about the early Africans in America, even their initial status in Virginia. Whether they were fully chattel slaves or servants is still sometimes debated by historians.

Another historical curiosity about the early arrivals is that many of the first Black people in America had European names on arrival, suggesting that they had not traveled directly from Africa but had spent some time enslaved in the West Indies prior to coming to America. It is also possible that they were what some historians have referred to as *Atlantic Creoles*. Atlantic

Creoles were Black people, sometimes of mixed ethnic ancestry, whose cultural fluidity, intelligence, and knowledge of different cultures gave them advantages in the New World. By the 1640s, some of the early arrivals had gained their freedom and continued to call themselves by their new names.[4]

Ultimately, faith played a crucial role, imbuing African Americans with a new identity and a "language" to speak and think about their communities. Faith gave them hope. The Christian faith played a central role in uniting Black peoples of many different ethnicities.

Revolutionary Faith and a Developing American Nation

Faith, politics, and the Enlightenment provided the intellectual framework for the Revolutionary War. Although some Black Americans were Christians in the early colonial period, the First Great Awakening (1730s and 1740s) brought more into the Church. Originating in Britain in the early 1730s, this movement of revivals quickly crossed the Atlantic. Leaders in the Great Awakening in the colonies included England's George Whitefield and American-born Jonathan Edwards. They, along with other Christian leaders, encouraged people in the colonies to convert, reconnect, and renew their relationship with Christ.

Preachers of the gospel wanted adherents to help restore the church to its evangelical roots of individual salvation, equality, and piety. Interested in experiencing what all the excitement was about, Benjamin Franklin decided to visit one of Whitefield's revivals in 1739, in Philadelphia. Although Franklin was not an orthodox Christian, the power of Whitefield's preaching left an impression on him. For attendees, the choice to go to a revival service could be somewhat risky socially, in that they could lose their standing in their homes or communities. Whitefield had few friends among local clergy, who did not support his style of preaching. Indeed, the local establishment often banished Whitefield from preaching at local churches. This meant that Whitefield often had to preach at local farms and in pastures. And people still came by the thousands, and many were converted. Outside the grasp of the formalized church structures, in those fields and pastures, locals expressed themselves in different ways. They raised their hands and shouted. They promised to live better lives.[5]

As Franklin listened to Whitefield preach on that farm in 1739, he witnessed the impact Whitefield's sermons had on people. He saw the expressions on their faces that indicated God was transforming their lives. This was different from the traditional Calvinism Franklin was raised in or the hierarchical Anglican religion he would have been familiar with. And yet he was inspired by it and by the sincerity of those gathered.

What he witnessed was not a distant faith where people attended church as a debt and little else. He encountered something that was personal and transformative. Something entirely democratic. People from all backgrounds gathered in the field together with one accord and were not separated by class or status. They then left the revival, devoted to changing their lives and spreading the Word of God. Franklin wrote,

> It was wonderful to see the Change soon made
> in the Manners [behavior] of our Inhabitants;

> from being thoughtless or indifferent about Reli-
> gion, it seem'd as if all the World were growing
> Religious; so that one could not walk thro' the
> Town in an Evening without Hearing Psalms
> sung in different Families of every Street.[6]

The Methodist, Baptist, and Presbyterian denominations in the American colonies all experienced growth in their membership because of the evangelical revivals. This ecumenical faith often led to a number of actions that were radical for the period. For example, some churches broke down race and class boundaries as their pastors and leaders condemned slavery. The evangelical message of equality even led men like Robert Carter, a prominent Virginia slave owner who converted to the faith, to manumit their slaves.[7]

As a result of the impact of evangelical Christianity, some African Americans attended integrated churches while others formed their own independent churches, such as the First Baptist Church in Williamsburg, Virginia. Others wanted to unite a broader coalition of Black Christians. For example, the Free African Society—which we will talk about later—was formed in Philadelphia in 1787 by Black people who wanted to host nondenominational religious meetings.

As Black people converted to the Christian faith in larger numbers, they solidified an evangelical identity. In many respects, this vision sounds similar to the one John Winthrop spoke about more than one hundred years earlier as the Puritans embarked for Massachusetts Bay.

As they prepared to leave their home in England, the Puritans gathered at church to worship God. Filled with enthusiasm about the opportunity to establish a community of believers, Winthrop rose at Holyrood Church in Southampton, England,[8] to encourage the men and women who would soon join him on the journey to "walk humbly with our God" and to "uphold a familiar commerce together in all meekness, gentleness, patience and liberality."[9] Not knowing what was to come or even if he would survive the trip, Winthrop was convinced that God was going to bless their community and establish it as a "City on a Hill."

Early African American Christian leaders wanted this too. Inspired by their faith and their desire to draw closer to each other, they became the living embodiment of America's early spiritual pioneers.

Listening to and following God's plan for our life is never easy because God often asks us to do things that are in opposition to the ways we normally want to act and live.

We can learn much from the past and from the way leaders of the past addressed the problems of their generation. Indeed, African Americans during this early period had to ask very difficult questions as they tried to follow Christ.

How did faith help African Americans overcome difficulty in the colonial period? In particular, we will examine the lives of Cyrus Bustill and Phillis Wheatley. Their lives serve as beacons of inspiration for all Christians and especially for those who want to unite people across the barriers that divide us. As we read about their faith, let us consider ways we can enhance our individual faith and the ways we may emulate the lives of believers who paved a road we can follow.

Cyrus Bustill: Faith and Slavery

A lack of sources for the period makes it difficult for a full examination of the faith early African American Christians practiced. Thankfully, by the time of the American Revolution, we have more documentation detailing their experiences. These resources are a blessing to the Christian reader because they provide important nuggets of wisdom and inspiration.

Cyrus Bustill is the first African American we will profile. Throughout his life, Bustill worked hard to be diligent, loving, and forgiving in his acts. His desire to forgive even extended to those who oppressed him.

We know little about his ancestry. Born a slave in 1732 in Burlington, New Jersey, Bustill was probably of mixed ancestry. Initially the property of Samuel Bustill, he was sold at a young age to a man named John Allen. Although Bustill later stated that Allen and his wife wanted to free him, the family's financial situation after John Allen's death was apparently so bad that they felt unable to do so because they needed him to help care for Allen's widow.

While we do not know what type of work Bustill did, it is possible that the family hired him out. *Hiring out* was an arrangement where masters hired their slaves to another person for cash. If this was true, this status granted Bustill more freedom than that of the typical field hand. Even though Bustill wanted to be free, he did not hold any anger toward Allen or his wife for not freeing him.[10]

Bustill understood the precariousness of his status as a slave and the limited control he had over his life. Bustill's status as a "favored" slave soon deteriorated. In Bustill's case, this

> **THROUGHOUT HIS LIFE, BUSTILL WORKED HARD TO BE DILIGENT, LOVING, AND FORGIVING IN HIS ACTS. HIS DESIRE TO FORGIVE EVEN EXTENDED TO THOSE WHO OPPRESSED HIM.**

occurred when he became the property of his master's son, who eventually sold him. While Bustill once had hopes of freedom, his dreams had taken a bad turn.

Even though times may seem dark, God always answers our prayers. Bustill found the strength to look beyond his situation. Indeed, deliverance was right in front of him. Thomas Pryor, his new master, was a devout Quaker who lived out his faith. When Pryor purchased Bustill, Pryor agreed to free him after seven years. While some may question Pryor's devotion to his faith because he kept Bustill enslaved for seven additional years, it is important to realize that it was normal for Quaker owners not to free their slaves until they had mastered a skilled trade. In this way, an enslaved person once freed would have the ability to take care of himself or herself. Bustill noted that during the last years of his enslavement, Pryor trained him to be a baker.

Pryor probably gave Bustill a lot of freedoms during these last years, and his enslavement was in name only. Nevertheless, as someone who had received promises before, only to be sold, Bustill wanted *legal* freedom. A very determined and principled man, Bustill also refused to marry while he was enslaved because he "would not perpetuate a race of slaves."[11] Bustill's desire to be legally free would validate a future marriage. Only freedom could promise him that he could not be separated from his family.

Legal freedom would also allow him to own his own bakery. While the cakes and bread that Bustill made with his hands and labor provided him a living, he understood that only freedom would give him full control of his labor and the proceeds from it—rather than it being granted to him through the benevolence of his master. Without documents attesting to his freedom, the dough that he kneaded for his bread and the delicious pastries he baked in his master's oven could easily be taken from him. Indeed, we cannot even be sure that the money he earned from his bakery ever went into his pockets. And if all or some of the money did go to him, such an arrangement with his master could be taken away anytime.

Bustill used these last years of enslavement to his advantage. When freedom came, he was prepared. He would marry a woman named Elizabeth Morey, a Native American woman from the Delaware tribe. With his wife, he moved from New Jersey to Philadelphia and opened a local bakery. In Philadelphia, the Bustills raised eight children. He was finally free to make his own money, worship in the place he wanted, and raise his children the way he and his wife desired.[12]

Philadelphia was a good place for a free African American like Bustill to live. With good business prospects and numerous social contacts available to him, Bustill quickly immersed himself in this small but prominent African American community of artisans, intellectuals, and businesspersons. This community not only included free men, but it also included slaves.

Race relations in Philadelphia were also better than in most other places at the time. Many free African American leaders in Philadelphia, particularly businessmen such as James Forten and William Gray, had established strong relationships with local white leaders, including Benjamin Rush and Benjamin Franklin. These relationships provided economic, social, and economic opportunities.

Benjamin Franklin and Benjamin Rush belonged to the Pennsylvania Abolition Society, the first society in America that advocated for the abolition of slavery. Founded primarily by local Quakers, the organization also helped African Americans increase their economic and social standing. This included supporting schools and helping African Americans find employment in the city.[13]

Bustill worked closely with prominent Quaker activists to help establish a society for African Americans. Free African Americans wanted to be independent and establish a mutual aid society that would help their brothers and sisters in need regardless of whether they were free or enslaved. Not only did the leaders of the Black community want to create an organization to help others; they also wanted a place of worship. The society they created, the Free African Society, united the African American communities' desire to worship God, while elevating the position of their community.

As the first Black religious institution in the city, the Free African Society provided a space that was autonomous. In time, the Free African Society would lead to the creation of the first Black Episcopal church, the African Episcopal Church of St. Thomas (Philadelphia, Pennsylvania), and the entire African Methodist

Episcopal denomination. Bustill, a slave for the majority of his life, along with Absalom Jones—who became the first African American to be ordained as a bishop in the Episcopal Church of the United States—became one of the founders of the African Episcopal Church of St. Thomas.[14]

Staying with Jesus in Times of Sorrow

Several months after helping found the Free African Society, Bustill delivered a speech to local African Americans titled "An Address to the Blacks in Philadelphia." This is one of the only direct sources we have that gives us a glimpse of this great man's personal faith. From the text of the speech, we know he was primarily interested in speaking to those still enslaved.

In 1787, when Bustill stood before the congregation of enslaved people gathered at the home of Richard Allen, who would later become the first bishop of the African American Methodist Episcopal denomination, Bustill did so at a time of tremendous change in Philadelphia. As a result of the work of friends in the Pennsylvania Abolition Society, the state had passed an abolition bill in 1780 that effectively laid the groundwork for abolishing slavery in the state. This was an important step. However, because the law focused on gradual emancipation, it freed only children of slave mothers born after 1780. Slaves born before this period would remain enslaved, perhaps for the remainder of their lives.

Knowing that some of the adults in attendance might never become free had to be difficult for Bustill. As someone who knew slavery and who had even refused to marry because of his hatred for the institution, he had to be somewhat disappointed that the Gradual Abolition Act of 1780 kept so many persons enslaved. During his almost forty years of enslavement, Bustill had relied on his faith to get him through the most difficult times. As he stood before his enslaved brothers and sisters, he had to find the strength to encourage them to first seek to be free in Christ and to ask God for the power to survive enslavement.

Bustill's desire to speak to enslaved people at the Free African Society demonstrated his desire to work with the larger Black community. Perhaps Bustill and the members of the Free African Society feared that a divide between free African Americans and slaves might develop as some free African Americans could begin to feel superior to slaves. Even though Bustill by this time in his life was one of the most prominent Black men in the city, he saw his manumission and prosperity not of his own doing but as part of God's plan. For someone of Bustill's stature in the community to affirm this equality among all was strong confirmation to the entire community that class distinctions had no place.[15]

Even though Bustill understood that some of the slaves he was speaking to might never become free, he wanted to encourage them to be prepared for freedom. Bustill told them about his experiences as a slave. As he spoke, he may have even reflected on how he perfected his recipes and properly heated the stove he baked bread in. He certainly pondered the connections he made with people who could help him in freedom. But as Bustill prepared his speech, he had to remember the reality that, had he not prepared properly for freedom while enslaved, he probably would not have had the opportunity to speak on behalf of the Free African Society that day.

Just as it was in Bustill's life, we must also prepare for our blessings. We can also risk losing them. In our lives, while the Lord is always opening doors, are we prepared to receive them? Bustill wanted the slaves who heard his voice to press forward and not to allow their current status to deter their commitment to preparing for their future.

After encouraging the slaves gathered to prepare for freedom, he still told them about the importance of forgiving those who were oppressing them. For Bustill this forgiveness did not mean that the person who forgave acquiesced to slavery, nor did the enslaved believe that the enslaver was superior. As an established member of the community, Bustill likely reflected on his past life, opening windows into his prior pain and feelings of insecurity. Surely, he had times of doubt and anger about his situation. Yet, he found the strength to overcome the anger for those who he felt had deceived him. How was he able to forgive the people who had enslaved him until he was thirty-seven years old? As he noted in his speech, he was able to do so by remembering that any blessing he had came from God, even his freedom.

This is why it is important to remember the Author of our blessings. Bustill did not tell those gathered that he was freed because of his own work, but that he was freed through God's intervention: "when it pleased him out of his Great Mercy and his Still abounding Goodness, to Pluck me out of the hands of unreasonable men, and at a time when I little expected it."[16] Bustill relied on his own experiences to encourage the slaves gathered to love their masters, to be ready for their deliverance, and to trust that God would act on the desires of their hearts.

Today it is difficult to understand how Bustill could encourage service to a master as a duty. Yet while he was a slave—even though he wanted to be free—Bustill saw it as his duty to be "faithful to your masters, at all times and on occasions, too, for this is Praise worthy, be honest and true to their intrust." [17] Bustill wanted those who remained enslaved to know that they could still exercise their power by rendering service in humility and by modeling Christian character to an earthly master. By rendering service, that person placed his or her Christian status above any other status, whether free or enslaved.

Bustill believed that all Christians must place their Christian identity first before every other identity or status. Bustill reminded everyone gathered that "God is no respecter of Persons, but in every nation, he, that feareth him and worketh righteousness, is accepted with him, and now my fellow men here is encouragement for us in particular to keep that in our favor which he hath so bountifully bestowed on us."[18]

To Bustill, all men were equal. Considering that this was a time of extreme racial and class bigotry, Bustill's declaration was radical. He hoped that his words could inspire and put the slaves in attendance on a path to self-actualization and liberation from the psychological damage slavery and racism caused. For Bustill, even illiteracy should not lead to negative emotions. Although many African Americans could not read or write, he implored them not to use this as cause to think less of themselves, or to separate from God.

As we reflect on Cyrus Bustill, let us be reminded that he upheld the Lord's words in the gospel of John to "Love one another. As I have loved you, so you must love one another. By this everyone will know that you are my disciples, if you love one another" (John 13:34–35).

How does this message resonate today? For me, I'm forced to think about my faith in dark times. Dark times can be difficult situations or relationships, each amounting to a barrier to moving forward. Bustill's radical faith in dark times is an example of what we call *unshakable faith*—a faith that allows us to push beyond the plateaus in our lives. Yes, it is hard to love the people who hurt us. Yes, it is hard sometimes to even love ourselves. Yes, it is hard to open ourselves up again after being hurt. But this is what our faith asks us to do. Cyrus Bustill, a man enslaved for more than half his life, who had experienced the ups and tremendous downs of life, demonstrates to us the redemptive power that can be accessed through this type of faith. He accessed that grace by not only acknowledging his past but also because he did not allow the memories of his past to prevent him from forgiving others and seeking redemption. Because he did that, he could press forward.

What an amazing message for us today. As we prayerfully seek to draw closer to the Lord daily, we will need to find the strength to forgive and, if possible, reconcile with those who have hurt us. In order to do that, we must be ready to open ourselves to each other, to press forward in Christ, and to move beyond the things that hold us back.

Loving our neighbors, regardless of who or what they are, is just as radical and tough today as it was during Jesus's time. Even if we are rejected in our attempts at being reconcilers, the important thing is that we make the attempt with sincerity. Loving and living according to Christ's call can transform even the hardest heart. Indeed, Bustill's descendant Anna Bustill Smith writes that Richard Pryor, the son of Bustill's former master, stated that Bustill's "deportment was solid and edifying . . . the inner man was transferred by renewing of the Holy Ghost."[19] As we can see here, Bustill's faith had an impact even on those who owned him. As we have seen with Paul, Philemon, and Onesimus, the faith of marginalized people has the power to transform lives and help to break down the barriers that divide us. For everyone, faith is the blessed assurance that all have a role to play in the kingdom of God and that He has blessed every one of us with the free will to follow Him.

Phillis Wheatley: Believing in God's Providence and Grace

Scholars know a lot more about the life of Phillis Wheatley compared to the life of Cyrus Bustill. As the first African American woman poet to be published in the United States, she is a historical icon. Today, many schools across America, particularly in traditionally African American neighborhoods, are named after her. At the same time, though her name is well known, most people know very little about her life. They know even less about the fact that much of Wheatley's poetry is an expression of her deep Christian faith.

In 1761, a young woman arrived in Boston on a slave ship named Phillis. In July of that year, prominent Boston merchant John Wheatley purchased her, replacing her given name lost to history with the name of the ship that brought her to America. He then provided her with the last name of his family. At the time he purchased her, John Wheatley judged her to be "between seven and eight Years of Age."[20]

We do not know what Phillis's real name was, or where she was from. We do know that Phillis Wheatley was born sometime around 1753 on the western coast of Africa. Other than a few short references in her poems to her parents and her homeland, we know nothing else about her years before her abduction. God only knows what Wheatley, a young girl separated from her family at such a young age, endured between her capture in Africa and her sale to John Wheatley. Young Phillis certainly carried psychological scars from her passage to America and from her first years here that might have destroyed most people. Perhaps she witnessed her parents die as she was taken from her community.

From her capture in Africa to her sale on the coast of Africa, she certainly saw a lot of death in her young life. This pathetic pattern of death continued through the Middle Passage, the journey of African slaves from Africa to the New World. According to Wheatley's biographer Vincent Carretta, only seventy-four of the ninety-five slaves who left Africa on the ship that brought her to America survived to their eventual sale in Boston.[21]

After her sale to John Wheatley, she endured *seasoning. Seasoning* is a term that refers to the period, typically about a year, when the slave was transitioned into their new life as a slave. This was a devastating period, as it was a mental and psychological destruction of everything the African once knew. Many masters repeatedly beat their slaves to force them to adapt to their new status. Not surprisingly, slaves often contracted diseases, and many died during seasoning.

Nonetheless, during this most traumatic period for enslaved Africans, Phillis, a young woman stripped from parents, family, and community, somehow survived against such insurmountable odds.

Soon young Phillis's intellect captured her owners' attention. John Wheatley could hardly imagine how the skinny little girl he had purchased, who knew so little about her past, learned how to read and write within sixteen months of her arrival. Outside of that provided by her family, she advanced without any public education. Furthermore, Wheatley was not only able to read and write, but she also had the ability to comprehend the depths of extremely difficult prose and text.[22]

Faith was a centerpiece in the Wheatley household. They were Congregationalists, a denomination that comes directly from the Puritans. John Wheatley had initially purchased Phillis as a gift for his wife, Susanna. Susanna Wheatley's faith had sustained her through the difficult experiences in her life. Susanna had given birth to five children, but only two of them survived into adulthood. Fewer than ten years before Phillis arrived on a slave ship, Susanna suffered the death of her youngest child, a girl roughly the same age as Phillis when John Wheatley purchased her. While only a suspicion, it's believed Susanna, a woman still grieving the death of her youngest child, and Phillis, a young girl grieving for her parents, bonded over their shared experiences of loss.

Young Phillis's conditions of servitude were not typical. The Wheatleys became young Phillis's family, although she was their slave. They had genuine feelings for the young woman— feelings that appear to have transcended racial thinking. Phillis was closest to Susanna who, according to Phillis, treated her as a daughter. As a child separated from her own mother before the strongest ties between mother and child had developed, Susanna played a maternal role in Phillis's life. The feelings Phillis had for Susanna also seem to affirm that she saw her as a second mother. When Susanna Wheatley died in 1774, it devastated Phillis. Only a year after Susanna and John Wheatley had freed her, Phillis had to experience her free life without the woman who had looked after and protected her. Phillis thought back to those early days in America and found the strength to write a dedication to Susanna Wheatley:

> I have lately met with a great trial in the death of my mistress, let us imagine the loss of a Parent, Sister or Brother the tenderness of all these were united, in her,—I was a poor little outcast & stranger when she took me in, not only into her house but I presently became, a sharer in her most tender affections, I was treated by her more like her child than her servant, no opportunity was left unimprov'd, of giving me the best of advice, but in terms how tender! How engaging! This I hope ever to keep in remembrance.[23]

The Wheatleys' two surviving children, John and Nathaniel, also took part in educating Phillis. Indeed, her quick study helped bolster the Wheatleys' interest in helping Phillis pursue her intellectual interests. Phillis quickly became conversant in the debates over religion and slavery being discussed in

Boston. As she was in the rooms, studying and eating with her owners, Phillis shared some of the most intimate details of the Wheatleys' lives. As a privileged slave, she probably did some household chores but spent just as much time in conversation and study with the Wheatley family. She would have dressed in the same clothes as the women of the Wheatley household. Through household conversations and debates, she would have been influenced by their feelings about the growing tension between the colonies and England.

The Wheatleys certainly had conversations about slavery, even though Phillis was a slave. From those conversations, Phillis would have understood that the institution of slavery was being challenged even by people such as her owners. At the same time, it must have seemed a contradiction to talk about slavery and its immorality to the people who own you. As the period of the Revolution approached, many people in the colonies, influenced by the ideas of the Enlightenment and evangelical religion, freely expressed their opinion that slavery was morally wrong, even though most of them probably never considered a means to end the institution.[24]

During this period, Wheatley wrote a number of poems that would later become a part of her only published book, *Poems on Various Subjects, Religious and Moral*. Even though Wheatley was a slave at the time of its publication, John Wheatley freed her later that year. Several years later, she married a free Black man named John Peters.

Wheatley found out that life as a free African American had extraordinary challenges, even in a supposedly liberal town like Boston. The dresses she wore and the accommodations she lived in declined significantly. Her husband had difficulties finding work, as free African Americans often experienced. Employers often preferred having slaves work for them than free African Americans. Without stable income, the couple's lives descended into poverty. Sadly, Wheatley died in 1784, with little money and no security: a far cry from her earlier fame, success, and prosperity. But she died a free woman.[25]

A Special Friendship

In 1765, after only four years in America, Wheatley had written a letter to Reverend Samson Occom, an ordained Presbyterian minister. Even though roughly thirty years separated their births, the two Christians shared much in common. Wheatley was the first Black woman to publish her writings. Occom was the first Native American to publish in English. A member of the Mohegan nation, Occom had experienced the power of the Word after attending one of the great religious revivals during the First Great Awakening. Hearing the Word and converting to Christianity, Occom wanted to become a missionary. Eventually, he was ordained a Presbyterian minister and missionary. His missionary work brought him into contact with Susanna Wheatley, who shared an interest in sharing the gospel to all.

It is not surprising that Phillis Wheatley began her correspondence to a well-known Christian missionary only four years after arriving in America. Occom's friendship with Susanna Wheatley certainly brought him into contact with Phillis. Occom would have seen a kindred spirit in Wheatley. Like her, he had experienced tremendous loss during his life. As a member of the Mohegan nation, he personally witnessed land grants, issued by the colonial government of Connecticut to colonists, cede much of the land that his ancestors claimed had been promised to them through trust after the Pequot War. Occom speaks about the "wandering life" of desperation of the Mohegan nation in his autobiography. Without hope, and with land becoming less and less available, the Mohegan nation was in a free fall.

The gospel provided Wheatley and Occom an opportunity to increase their status, but it may have raised some questions. Both were passionate about their faith. But they also recognized the racial prejudice they lived with daily was a result of the unwillingness of many Christians to move beyond it. As a Native American who had witnessed the oppression of his people as well as the destruction of communities, Occom could identify with the plight of enslaved Africans. He could see the unequal pay he received throughout his ministry as compared to white ministers' as another consequence of prejudice.

By the 1770s, Occom's social views had led him to question slavery. He wrote a letter to Phillis Wheatley expressing his concerns about the institution and its impact on enslaved persons. Although this letter has not survived, Wheatley's response has. In it, it is clear that Occom's letter spoke of his low regard for ministers who held slaves. Considering Occom's experiences with white ministers who consistently ridiculed him and took advantage of him, it is not surprising that toward Occom's later years his social vision became more inclusive of the plight of slaves. Wheatley writes that she "was greatly satisfied with your reasons respecting the Negroes, and think highly reasonable what you offer in Vindication of their natural Rights."[26]

The friendship between Wheatley and Occom is important because it helped both recognize that they were not alone in their struggles. While many of the people they encountered in their lives may not have understood their deepest feelings and anxieties, it was important that they found others with whom they could speak and share freely.

Oppression Today

Just as Occom and Wheatley suffered oppression during their lives, many marginalized communities exist in our nation as a result of systemic racism and ethnic prejudice. In urban centers like Chicago and Baltimore, entire families are often trapped in crime-ridden neighborhoods where death is commonplace and hope is drained out by nihilism, or a belief that life has no meaning. In rural America, unemployment and opioid addiction have been rising, leaving a generation of people in danger of being lost. In the rural Deep South, many African Americans still remain in extreme poverty, a fact that has existed since the end of slavery. Health disparities that have persisted since the Civil War continue to plague African American communities. For example, our nation's health disparities have directly led to the higher mortality rates for African Americans during the COVID-19 outbreak.

As a nation, we pride ourselves on the idea of upward mobility but in reality social mobility both then as well as now is hard to achieve. The scars that poverty often inflicts can last generations. Both Occom and Wheatley connected because they were able to find the strength to trust God, which included strength to forgive their oppressors. Even then, they faced the consequences of systemic oppression.[27]

Occom and Wheatley's friendship was strengthened by the reality that neither had a relationship with Jesus during their early years but found God during periods of revival. Wheatley was also influenced by revivalist preachers, particularly George Whitefield. Similar to Occom, Wheatley saw her conversion as a result of God's providence, even if, ironically, the prejudice against her and other obstacles prepared the way for her salvation.

In Romans 8:28 Paul writes: "And we know that for those who love God all things work together for good, for those who are called according to his purpose" (ESV). Like Paul, Wheatley and Occom saw it as their mission in life to give back to oppressed people and their communities.

> **LIKE PAUL, WHEATLEY AND OCCOM SAW IT AS THEIR MISSION IN LIFE TO GIVE BACK TO OPPRESSED PEOPLE AND THEIR COMMUNITIES.**

Finding Her Voice

Phillis Wheatley placed God first in her life, a fact that helps us contextualize her views of her capture, sale, and introduction into slavery. This view is expressed in one of her poems:

> 'Twas mercy brought me from my Pagan land,
> Taught my benighted soul to understand
> That there's a God, that there's a *Savior* too:

Once I redemption neither fought nor knew,
Some view our sable race with scornful eye,
"Their color is a diabolic die."
Remember, *Christians*, *Negroes*, black as *Cain*,
May be refin'd, and join th'angelic train.[28]

It is important to highlight a few things. One, whatever obstacles Wheatley had to endure to get to know Jesus, she interpreted them as part of God's plan for her salvation. Two, even though she certainly carried scars from her past, she believed that she had gained Christ as a result of her suffering. Three, she believed that all Christians are asked to sacrifice for Christ.

In the aforementioned poem, Wheatley does not celebrate the institution of slavery, but rather she details her vision for a better America. One can imagine Phillis writing this poem in the home of her owners. Knowing that she was a slave as a result of her skin color, Wheatley scorns those who believed in the inferiority of Africans, rejecting the idea that the color of Africans makes them inferior. And yet Africans, including Wheatley, were condemned for their race. She then reminds the reader that everyone can "join th'angelic train."[29] One wonders if she had ever felt that the Wheatleys held prejudice against her because of her race. Perhaps in the many discussions she had with them, she felt a need to convince her own owners that she was equal to them. Whatever the case, Wheatley wanted to encourage the reader to welcome everyone into God's house, regardless of background.

Sharing the experiences of her life through her pen, Wheatley wrote passionately about prejudice and its consequences. As a Black child stripped from her parents and cast into slavery, her poetry was the only way she could tell the entire world about the horrors that had almost condemned her.

> I, young in life, by seeming cruel fate
> Was snatch'd from *Afric's* fancy'd happy seat:
> What pangs excruciating must molest,
> What sorrows labour in my parent's breast?
> Steel'd was that soul and by no misery mov'd
> That from a father seiz'd his babe belov'd:
> Such, such my case. And can I then but pray
> Others may never feel tyrannic sway?[30]

These lyrics provide a more nuanced understanding of Wheatley's views. On one hand, her faith helped her reconcile her pain that came from being separated from her birth parents. On the other hand, her faith provided her the opportunity to love those who caused her suffering. But Wheatley's writing also speaks to white people when she asks them to recognize the consequences of their racial prejudices. She tells them bluntly that their prejudice and racism was the cause of her pain. And that it was God alone who had helped sustain her in conditions that would have killed most people.

One of the challenges that Wheatley faced—also shared by people like Occom—was the reality that many of the people who introduced her to the gospel were slave owners or supporters of the institution. Even though they provided her education and the opportunity to publish, her owners were part of this group of slavers. Another example is the Reverend George Whitefield, whom she clearly saw as a spiritual mentor. By the time Wheatley heard Whitefield preach, he had turned away from his earlier antislavery message. One can imagine Wheatley listening to Whitefield's fiery sermons and feeling inspired by the Spirit. Yet, as she listened to him, she also realized that although his ministry was inclusive of everyone, he did not practice true equality but had accepted slavery as a just institution.

Even though Whitefield accepted slavery, Wheatley still opened her heart to Whitefield and was sincerely inspired by him in much the same way that Benjamin Franklin had been years earlier. Wheatley recognized that even if Whitefield's heart had hardened on the institution of slavery, he never stopped proclaiming the gospel to all people. In response to his death, she refers to his preaching "as music of thy (God's) tongue."[31] She reflected on Whitefield's sermons, writing:

> Take him, ye *Africans*, he longs for you,
> "*Impartial Saviour* is his title due:
> Wash'd in the fountain of redeeming blood,
> You shall be sons, and kings, and priests to God."[32]

Because Wheatley believed in the power of forgiveness and understanding, she was able to focus on the parts of Whitefield's sermons where he spoke about redemption, equality, and God's favor for Black people. Regardless of Whitefield's views on slavery and race, Wheatley saw him as a vehicle of God's providence. She recognized that no one is perfect and that God uses imperfect people to promote His kingdom.

Wheatley's words of forgiveness and understanding are as profound today. In our society, old divisions still seem difficult to bridge. We even have new divisions and more up-to-date means to express them. If we look at our media, politics, friendships, and even our churches, too many of us demand that people completely agree with us before we listen to them. People will *unfriend* you on social media if you disagree with them about anything. People from different political parties refuse to speak to one another. But Phillis Wheatley used her pen and prose to show her readers a more excellent way. The fact that she could listen to and recognize the words of a slave owner does not mean that she agreed with his position. Rather it means that she recognized a person's humanity in a damaged world. She also recognized that God can use imperfect people to bless others. We should all look at our lives and ask ourselves how many blessings have we missed because we have closed doors to our brothers.

Looking Forward to the Promises of Our Resurrection

Phillis Wheatley's belief in the resurrection helped her through periods of grief. Even though her last years were difficult, I am sure she found comfort in her faith.

Wheatley spoke a lot about grief in her poems. Indeed, many of her poems are elegies. Elegies are poetic reflections, typically over death or suffering. For example, in one of them she writes an elegy about a young child who had died. Adopting his voice, she says, "Thanks to my God, who snatch'd me to the skies." She ends this elegy with a picture of heaven, presenting it as "pleasures without measure, without end."[33]

For Wheatley, death was an escape from pain. In another poem about the death of another young child, she wrote:

She feels the iron hand of pain no more;
The dispensations of unerring grace,
Should turn your sorrows into grateful praise;
Let then no tears for her henceforward flow,
No more distress'd in our dark vale below.

Restrain your tears, and cease your plaintive moans.
Freed from a world of sin, and snares, and pain,
Why would you wish your daughter back again?[34]

It is important to point out that Wheatley was not saying that death should be sought as an escape from pain. To the contrary, she viewed death as part of God's divine plan that was to occur at His appointed time. Therefore, she ends the poem encouraging everyone to "Adore the God who gives and takes away; eye him in all, his holy name revere."[35]

Faith and Suffering

Romans 8:21 states "that the creation itself will be liberated from its bondage to decay and brought into the freedom and glory of the children of God." For Phillis Wheatley, someone who was captured and enslaved by a broken and corrupt system, her belief in the resurrection gave her hope.

Phillis Wheatley shared her experiences with us to demonstrate that life on Earth is temporal and always changing. Sitting down to share her experiences with the world, Wheatley wanted readers of her poems to remember that God is our Redeemer. Looking at her life and her trials and tribulations, she hoped that one day we would all acquire "a nobler title, and superior name!"[36]

> CREATION ITSELF WILL BE LIBERATED FROM ITS
> BONDAGE TO DECAY AND BROUGHT INTO THE
> FREEDOM AND GLORY OF THE CHILDREN OF GOD.
> (ROMANS 8:21)

Today, too many Christians seem to want to reject the reality that suffering is part of our Christian journey. Wheatley wanted her readers to recognize that Christ offers something great to those who persevere. Sadly, today it seems as if our inability to handle loss and pain may have contributed to the nation's mental health crisis, including the increased number of people struggling with addiction and suicidal ideation. To those who are suffering—Christ offers us comfort. Wheatley affirmed this reality by assuring us that we can embrace suffering and praise God at the same time. For example, she writes upon the death of a minister she respected:

> Great God, incomprehensible, unknown
> By sense, we bow at thine exalted throne.
> O, while we beg thine excellence to feel,
> Thy sacred Spirit to our hearts reveal,
> And give us of that mercy to partake,
> Which thou hast promis'd for the *Saviour's* sake![37]

Wheatley notes that when there are things we do not understand about God, the best posture before Him is one of humble trust. Because Wheatley understood grief and suffering firsthand, she was able to communicate her empathy with those in times of sorrow.[38]

Wheatley looked at the world and all its warts and still celebrated the beauty of God's creation. Marveling at God's handiwork, she looked forward to a day when everyone could freely take part in that creation:

> How *Jesus'* blood for your redemption flows.
> See him with hands out-stretcht upon the cross;
> Immense compassion in his bosom glows;
> He hears revilers, nor resents their scorn:
> What matchless mercy in the Son of God!
> When the whole human race by sin had fall'n,
> He deign'd to die that they might rise again,
> And share with him in the sublimest skies,
> Life without death, and glory without end.[39]

Wheatley revealed in this passage that she believed in redemption. To her redemption was something beautiful. Furthermore, she confirmed her belief that Jesus is the Son of God, that He was sent by the Father to atone for our sins, that He died on the cross, that He rose again, and that one day we will join Him. These facts have provided millions of Christians comfort. In that day—all who believe in Him will be united.

Both Cyrus Bustill and Phillis Wheatley endured tremendous obstacles during their lives, but they did not allow these obstacles to dilute their praise. They affirmed Jesus as our great Redeemer. Bustill and Wheatley understood that Jesus forgave us, even though we contributed to His death. Their inspirational lives encourage us to remember the Lord's words: "And when you stand praying, if you hold anything against anyone, forgive them, so that your Father in heaven may forgive you your sins" (Mark 11:25).

By thinking less about ourselves and taking up His cross, we as Christians can more boldly follow Him, and make the world better. During our journey, we place Christ above our personal desires and interests. We allow Christ to direct our interactions with the world. We realize that our responsibility to His creation is great.

Christians can seek justice by emulating Christ. Not for selfish reasons or to simply be considered on the "right side of history." True justice demands that we seek it for Jesus's sake, submitting ourselves to God's will and allowing Him to direct us in paths of righteousness with empathy, compassion, and understanding for all.

Explore Your Faith with Cyrus Bustill and Phillis Wheatley

* What can I do to reconcile with people who have caused me pain?

* As a Christian, how can I help bridge divisions along the lines of race, class, and ethnicity?

* How can I emulate Bustill's and Wheatley's faith by the way I live my life and approach my relationships?

CHAPTER 2

SONS AND DAUGHTERS OF THE AMERICAN REVOLUTION

Therefore everyone who hears these words of mine and puts them into practice is like a wise man who built his house on the rock. The rain came down, the streams rose, and the winds blew and beat against that house; yet it did not fall, because it had its foundation on the rock.

MATTHEW 7:24–25

Evangelical religion had radically transformed Cyrus Bustill's life in the years before and after the American Revolution. By 1800, however, the lack of progress in race relations left many Black Christians increasingly disillusioned.

This frustration is seen in the creation of the Free African Society. It is even more clear in the establishment of the Black Episcopal Church and the African Methodist Episcopal denomination; these were additional signs of broader trends that occurred during the early national period (from 1789 to 1837). Their founding was part of a pattern that continues to this day: African Americans define themselves as *American* and, at the same time, create a space for themselves to define what being *Black and American* truly means.

African American leaders like Absalom Jones and Richard Allen helped blaze the way for a more active and prophetic expression of African American evangelical Christianity. Cyrus Bustill reflected the views of an older generation that envisioned the erosion of the barriers between the races as a result of evangelical religion and other social transformation. Allen, Jones, and others witnessed the accelerating conservatism of an increasingly mainstream evangelical religion during the early national period that led to further segregation and racial oppression. Bustill's generation saw the revolutionary period lead to economic devastation and the decline of slavery as an economically viable institution, particularly in the upper South's tobacco-growing states. Allen, Jones and others witnessed Eli Whitney's cotton gin during the early nineteenth century make slavery stronger where slavery remained. Bustill had come of age during the Revolution, the First Great Awakening, and the

Enlightenment, a period of challenge to institutions and to traditional social relationships. Allen, Jones, and others saw political and social institutions strengthen and shut out Black people and diminish the few opportunities they had for social and economic advancement.

The changes Allen and Jones and Black people in general endured led to an increasingly awakened generation of Black men and women who wanted to expand on the legacy of the revolutionary period. Who believed that the only way to advance their status would be by forcefully pushing for economic, social, and spiritual change particularly in the North, but also in urban centers like Richmond and Charleston in the South. The growth of the free Black population undergirded this new radicalism, along with a devotion to community formation. Individuals from Black communities believed that through the intervention of Jesus Christ, and by devoting themselves to Him, they could help bring about the abolition of slavery.

Imbued by the spirit of the Revolution—and the devastating reality that the era of the American Revolution did not fully lead to the changes their predecessors had hoped for—a new generation of Black Americans began to examine, explore, and practice their Christian faith in ways that expanded on the social vision of their forefathers. Just as devout as the earlier generation, the new generation was much more persistent, typically through community activism, to pursue an agenda that specifically focused on addressing the issues that plagued Black communities. Slavery represented the major issue that demanded a response from the church. This new generation wanted more than people *believing* that slavery was wrong. They demanded immediate abolition. They pushed for Black agency—power—for people in the United States and abroad.

The Second Great Awakening

I often explore with others this irony: as Black people in America increasingly identified as *American,* the nation increasingly segregated and pushed them to the edges of American society. Perhaps nowhere was this segregation as profound as it was in the church. Frustrated by the racial segregation in many churches, the majority of African Americans established independent churches. These churches tended to align more closely (than the churches they had left) to the democratic and radical foundations of the First Great Awakening and the American Revolution.

If the First Great Awakening introduced many African Americans to the Christian faith, the Second Great Awakening brought even more people to the Lord. Beginning around 1790 and reaching an apex around 1830, this era led to a tremendous revival of faith: much larger and more significant than the First Great Awakening. Indeed, by the end of the Second Great Awakening in the 1850s, it is likely that most Black Americans had converted to Christianity.

Although we do not know all of the reasons that led to this second American religious awakening, it arose during a period of tremendous social, political, and economic transformation. Historically, periods of great transformation and displacement also witness periods of religious renewal. In this case, America was in its infancy as a nation.

The first decades of the nineteenth century ushered in a period of limitless expectations as America became more democratic, at least for white men. Immigrants came to the United States in larger numbers, often bringing with them different cultural values. The combination of industrial advances and migration brought thousands of people to the cities. These people left the countryside and the traditional family networks that existed there. As Americans sought to expand their territory, many residents moved south and west, extending our nation's borders.

Slavery was shifting too. In the North, the institution was on the road to complete extinction. In 1787, the United States Congress passed the Northwest Ordinance (encompassing territory west of the Appalachian Mountains and east of the Mississippi River), effectively banning slavery from ever existing there. Changes even came to the South. America's purchase of two regions—the Louisiana and Florida territories, in 1803 and in 1819, respectively—effectively expanded slavery. The acquisition of Texas in 1845 also extended slavery. Furthermore, as more people moved to Southern cities, slave masters experimented with the institution to see whether slavery could be as successful for them in urban centers as it was in rural spaces. Slavery proved flexible for industrial cities in the South.

Any time of transition creates uncertainty as people look for answers to navigate change. People want clarity. In a context of family disruptions, increasing immigration of people from different communities, and an industrial revolution, many Christian believers reflected on the meaning of their faith and life in the context of all the change. Not surprisingly, many men and women wondered if the world was ending. Indeed, even though the prospects for America overall remained bright, America's transitions during the period from 1810 to 1850 demanded a lot of adaptation.

Theologically, American Christians responded by embracing a more engaged form of Protestant evangelicalism. Since the First Great Awakening, evangelical Christians had pondered their role in society. Although Christian ministers such as George Whitefield and Jonathan Edwards spoke about conversion and evangelism, they still held to the ideas of predestination and the total depravity of humanity. Additionally, their views did not lean toward free will (the ability of the individual to change his or her life and those of others). George Whitefield asserted that only God had the power to change and alter a person.[1] Whitefield continued this theme in one of his sermons: "The Seed of the Woman and the Seed of the Serpent," based on Genesis 3:15, and published in 1742.

> That they can do nothing of or for themselves and should therefore come to God, beseeching them to give them faith, by which they will then show forth by their works, out of love and gratitude to the ever blessed Jesus, their most glorious Redeemer, for what he has done for their souls.[2]

As we can see, Whitefield denies the individual the ability to do anything for himself or herself or to change his or her own status except through divine intervention. By the early nineteenth century, however, many American Christians were moving away from this perspective in a rapidly transforming nation.

In nineteenth-century America, the upheaval of both the social and spiritual landscapes ignited a growing receptivity to new religious worldviews. One worldview being that individuals have free will. During this period in America, particularly in the North, many people moved away from traditional Calvinism by embracing an ideology of *free will*. In this theological iteration, often referred to as *Arminianism,* God's grace provides us with the ability to reject or accept His invitation. This theological outlook certainly fit with the realities of the new American landscape—one where people had more opportunity to create their own destinies. The theology of free will infused Americans, slave and free, with a sense of destiny and limitless potential.

The implications extended beyond religious matters. If people have free will in matters of their eternal salvation, then perhaps they could leave home to follow their earthly dreams. Perhaps slaves could escape from their masters. Perhaps masters could transform traditional master-and-slave relationships too. Indeed, free will had far-reaching implications by placing more power in the hands of individuals.

Postmillennialism is the second theological theme during the early nineteenth century. Revelation 20:1–3 refers to a thousand-year period, the millennium, when Satan will be bound. Those who hold a postmillennial view of Christ's return (the return of Christ after this era) see the work of the church as a prelude to this period of peace and tranquility. Therefore, the revivals of the period were not only about reviving one's soul, but also about preparing society for the millennium and, after that, Christ's return.[3]

To the postmillennialist, faith meant much more than personal conversion and salvation. Postmillennialists believe that the individual has a larger role to play in society—individuals can transform it to prepare for the millennium. Their job is to help the society make changes to eradicate sin in order for the millennium to begin. People did not have to look far to find the ills of society to correct. Postmillennialists would lead the most important social movements of the era, including the temperance, education, and women's rights movements. Abolition of slavery was another of these social movements. By the 1830s, postmillennial Christians led that movement too.

It is an interesting historical curiosity that postmillennialism and the religious revivals had an impact on both the anti-slavery and proslavery movements. The church has always harbored differences, some large and others less so. For example, different interpretations over the end times, while important, are not issues that should lead to division. However, American slavery and racism were issues of grave concern. Even now, the church struggles over issues of ethnicity and race.

The important thing to do when we are divided over these major issues is to focus on the things that unite us. The Bible is our guidebook because it is God's Word.

When the church is divided, Christians should act on principle in order to settle our differences, recognizing the catastrophic consequences if we hold to unbiblical positions. For example, believing that Jesus is a member of one particular political party or another is one way this happens. Racial prejudice is another unbiblical perspective. Throughout history, we have seen how these divisions hurt the church. This happened

> **THE IMPORTANT THING TO DO WHEN WE ARE DIVIDED OVER THESE MAJOR ISSUES IS TO FOCUS ON THE THINGS THAT UNITE US. THE BIBLE IS OUR GUIDEBOOK BECAUSE IT IS GOD'S WORD.**

during the early nineteenth century when Christians allowed their prejudices to muddy their interpretation of God's Word. Sadly, prejudice kept many Christians from experiencing the fullness of the gospel. This still happens today.

Ultimately, the ideologies of free will and postmillennialism influenced both the proslavery and antislavery movements. Proslavery advocates embraced the institution as a positive good for society, believing they could achieve God's will by merely introducing slaves to the slavers' own interpretation of the Bible.

Many Southern intellectuals advocated that slavery was part of a reciprocal relationship between masters and slaves. These intellectuals included William A. Smith, a Methodist preacher and president of Randolph-Macon College in Virginia. He argued that masters have obligations to their slaves because, "Each one is held to a strict accountability for the faithful performance of his duty, the one to the other—'for there is no respect of persons with God.'"[4] Smith also believed that since masters provided clothing for their slaves and introduced them to the gospel, slaves would owe masters their service for life.

The Scriptures and history have proven the interpretations of Smith and others wrong. Even though they were wrong, the *churches* many masters created for slaves thrived. As plantation churches emerged throughout the South, these bodies, even though often practicing a watered-down and proslavery interpretation of the gospel, helped spread the good news of Jesus Christ throughout the southern territories.

The New African American Resistance

For most evangelical abolitionists, slavery was a sin that could prevent the millennium from happening. In addition to slavery being a moral wrong, Black abolitionists in particular had other reasons to be concerned. Although basically extinct in the North, between 1810 and 1860, America's slave population increased from a little more than one million to roughly four million!

Whereas African Americans during the era of the American Revolution had reason to believe that slavery was on a path toward extinction, those hopes had largely died by the 1830s. As religious leaders like Nat Turner and David Walker surveyed slavery and the plight of Black people, they saw violent revolution as the only way to end slavery. In 1843, Henry Highland Garnet, a Black Presbyterian minister, argued that if Black people truly wanted to be free that they "themselves must strike the blow!"[5]

Garnet's words echoed those of Nat Turner and David Walker, who came before him.

In 1831, Nat Turner led a slave rebellion in Southampton County, Virginia. A favored slave on his plantation, Turner, who knew how to read and write, was also a minister. With a small group of supporters, he led a rebellion that left more than fifty white people dead. In the aftermath of the rebellion, Turner escaped capture for roughly six weeks. After his capture, he was thrown in prison where he faced certain death. A week later, he was tried and sentenced to death.

No one knew what led Turner to lead the rebellion until a lawyer named Thomas R. Gray showed up to get his statement. While the accuracy of Gray's account has been questioned by some, I do not believe we can or should dismiss this, the only account we have that purports to come from Nat Turner:

> I had too much sense to be raised, and if I was, I would never be of any use to any one as a slave. Now finding I had arrived to man's estate, and was a slave, and these revelations being made known to me, I began to direct my attention to this great object, to fulfil the purpose for which, by this time, I felt assured I was intended.[6]

> **"I BEGAN TO DIRECT MY ATTENTION TO THIS GREAT OBJECT, TO FULFIL THE PURPOSE FOR WHICH, BY THIS TIME, I FELT ASSURED I WAS INTENDED. "**
> **—NAT TURNER**

In his "confessions," as Gray called them, taken just before his execution, Nat Turner expressed his belief in free will and postmillennial ideology. Even as he knew that he would be sentenced to death for leading the rebellion, Turner defiantly told

Gray—who seems to mock Turner's attempt at revolt, given that the penalty for it would be death—that his enslavement prevented him from his *purpose*. As a postmillennialist, Turner had a responsibility to try to destroy what kept him from doing God's will. Chained in a small and filthy prison cell, tired and beaten, Turner still stood on his principle, no matter what would happen to him. He told Thomas R. Gray:

> For as the blood of Christ had been shed on this earth, and had ascended to heaven for the salvation of sinners, and was now returning to earth again in the form of dew—and as the leaves on the trees bore the impression of the figures I had seen in the heavens, it was plain to me that the Saviour was about to lay down the yoke he had borne for the sins of men, and the great day of judgment was at hand.

Turner's statement reveals that he saw his actions in terms of their potential impact on ushering in the end times. Even though he knew he was going to be executed for his actions, Turner held firm to his faith and his belief in the millennium.[7]

While it is difficult for Christians to support the violent measures adopted by Turner and others, it is hard not to recognize just how bleak life was for a slave like Nat Turner.

Evangelical religion permeated the foundations of the anti-slavery movement. Turner and most African Americans of the period agreed that abolition (the belief that slavery needed to end immediately) was a social movement they needed to embrace. Some white northerners were also abolitionists or leaned strongly toward it. Yet others found a middle ground. Unable to fully embrace antislavery, they supported colonization: removing free African Americans from the American continent.

Creating a New Nation

While colonization found strong support in the white community, only a few African Americans supported it. It is not difficult to understand why so few African Americans supported colonization. The vast majority of African Americans at that time saw America as their home and did not believe that they should be expected to leave America so that they could be treated fairly. They wanted to stand and fight for their rights *in* America.

A small number of African Americans did see benefits in leaving America. Paul Cuffee, an early supporter of colonization, was an African American businessman. Cuffee was involved in maritime trade and owned his own ship. He traveled and conducted business all along the Atlantic coast. In 1812 Cuffee visited Freetown, a town in Sierra Leone settled by freed slaves. As a businessman, Cuffee wanted to establish trade relationships between African Americans and Africans that could benefit both groups. For Cuffee, colonization was not something that all African Americans needed to do. But he believed that colonizing Africa could help establish connections between Black Americans and Africans.

Cuffee was also an early supporter of a form of Black nationalism, the belief that Black people need to be empowered and create networks for self-sufficiency. Cuffee encouraged Black Americans to understand "that sobriety and steadfastness, with all faithfulness, be recommended, so that professors may be examples in all things; doing justly, loving mercy, and walking humbly." For Cuffee, colonization was an option for African Americans who did not want to wait for justice. At the same time, he also saw emigration to Africa as an opportunity for Black people to minister to and assist their brothers and sisters who lived there. He said, "I have for these many years past felt a lively interest in [the Africans'] behalf, . . . wishing that the inhabitants of the colony might become established in the truth, and thereby be instrumental in its promotion amongst our African brethren."[8]

The American Colonization Society (ACS) was the American organization most involved in assisting Black people to emigrate to Africa. Today the ACS is often viewed as an organization that not only had little support in the Black community but also was one organized and influenced by people whose primary goal was to convince free Black people to leave the United States. There is some truth in this assertion since many of the leaders of the ACS cared very little for helping Blacks who were enslaved.

However, it is also true that some Black people saw the ACS as a legitimate option not only to escape racism but also to help prepare the way for the kingdom of God in Africa. For these reasons, some African Americans were willing to work with the ACS.

Robert Finley, a Presbyterian minister, founded the ACS in 1816 with the intent to establish a colony in Africa, which freed slaves could colonize. Although Finley held some prejudice against Black people, he sincerely wanted to do something to ameliorate America's race problem and particularly the condition of African Americans.

Finley did not believe that slavery was a just institution. And because of the harm America caused Black people, Finley argued that sending Black people to Africa could help "repair the injuries inflicted by our fathers."[9] He envisioned the ACS as a political body that could encourage state legislatures to pass laws to encourage the emancipation of slaves on the condition that they be transferred to Africa immediately thereafter: "By these means the evil of slavery will be diminished, and in a way so gradual as to prepare the whites for the happy and progressive change."[10]

Finley was also an early advocate of *moral suasion. Moral suasion* is a term that defines the ways social reformers of this period appealed to society's moral compass to support their causes. Appealing to the Christian sensibilities of white and Black people, Finley argued that colonization was a means to improve the morality of both groups.[11] As a white man who had an understanding of America's past and present, Finley concluded that Black people could never achieve equal status in America. For Finley the division between the races was too great. Moreover, he did not think that white Americans would ever accept Black people as full participants in society. In this sense, he believed that it was unfair to Black people for them to

> "BY THESE MEANS THE EVIL OF SLAVERY WILL BE DIMINISHED, AND IN A WAY SO GRADUAL AS TO PREPARE THE WHITES FOR THE HAPPY AND PROGRESSIVE CHANGE. "
> —ROBERT FINLEY

remain in America. African Americans "will be kept down, on the one side by prejudice, too deep rooted to be eradicated, on the other, by the recollection of former inferiority, and despair of ever assuming an equal standing in society."[12]

Although Finley and some of the other supporters of the ACS did not always have the most altruistic reasons for pushing for colonization, it would be a mistake to say that all of them had bad intentions. Nor is it helpful to see the Black people who worked with the ACS as merely misled or duped into leaving America. For African American supporters, colonization represented an opportunity for them to uphold the promises of the American Revolution and to establish a kingdom for God as they brought a revival to the African continent.

Lott Cary: Slavery to Freedom

Lott Cary was perhaps the most important Black missionary during the early nineteenth century. Born a slave around 1780 in Charles City, Virginia, a community roughly thirty miles south of Richmond, he was raised in a Baptist household. According to tradition, his parents and grandmother were devout Christians. Like many slaves in rural areas near urban centers, his master hired him out in the city.

Cary's master hired him to a tobacco warehouse where he was soon promoted to be a manager. Even by this time, Richmond was a leading producer of tobacco. Tobacco warehouses emerged throughout the city, and many managers of the warehouses hired slaves to work there. As one of the few Black managers, Cary made good money, some he kept for himself.

An entrepreneurial businessman, Cary supplemented this income by packaging and selling the waste tobacco from the warehouse. Cary had many reasons to try to earn as much money as he could. He was a married man with two children, and he had a dream to purchase his freedom and that of his entire family. Sadly, his wife died in 1813, a few months before he was able to purchase her. He was, however, able to purchase his own freedom and that of his two children.

Cary dedicated his life to Christ and was baptized at the First Baptist Church in Richmond. Although most of the congregation was white, it did provide services for Black people. Not long after his baptism, he became a minister, "holding meetings and exhorting among the colored people."[13] Along with William Crane, a white shoemaker and businessman who had an interest in promoting the Black community, Cary established a separate ministry for African Americans at the First Baptist Church, which had roughly one thousand African American members at that time.

Around 1816, Cary and Crane established the Richmond African Baptist Missionary Society. As Cary and Crane planned to spread the gospel to Africa, they also thought of ways to help Black people in America. Both members of the First Baptist Church in Richmond, the two men shared a love of God that linked them across the barriers that divided them. Certainly, the two men prayed and worshiped together. As they did, they continued to work to make Richmond a better place for African Americans. They also established a Black school that met three times a week. Both men—Cary, an African American, and Crane, a white man—were helping the African American community.[14]

Cary saw African missions as a way to establish more free- dom over his life. He did not see colonization as a scheme to remove free Black people like him from America.

Cary was extremely successful in Richmond. In a short time, he had purchased his freedom and was making good money as a manager of a tobacco warehouse. He also married again and purchased a farm in Henrico County for $1,500, almost twice the amount that it took to purchase his family out of slavery. He was so well respected at his job that his employer offered to pay him a yearly salary of $1,000 if he remained in Richmond.[15]

Cary was not forced out of America—he left willingly because of his love of Christ and his desire to help people come to the Lord. He told his friend William Crane, "I feel bound to labor for my suffering race."[16] At the same time, he expressed his eth- nic pride saying that he had "been determined for a long time to go to Africa and at least to see the country for myself."[17] Going to Africa would allow him to help his people both in America and in Africa.

Perhaps it is best to see Lott Cary and the people who left Virginia with him as similar to the Puritans of the seventeenth century. Both groups viewed emigration as a solution to their persecution in their homeland. Even though the land they

CARY SAW AFRICAN MISSIONS AS A WAY TO ESTABLISH MORE FREEDOM OVER HIS LIFE. HE DID NOT SEE COLONIZATION AS A SCHEME TO REMOVE FREE BLACK PEOPLE LIKE HIM FROM AMERICA.

would gain in Africa would need to be developed, Cary believed that Africa provided empowerment to those who would leave with him. As he prepared to leave Richmond, he gave one final sermon at his home church.

Speaking at a pulpit at the First Baptist Church near the James River where he would begin his journey to Africa, he told the people gathered that he was "an African, and in this country, however meritorious my conduct, and respectable my character, I cannot receive the credit due to either." Cary hoped to establish an American colony in Africa where he could be "estimated by my merits" and not, according to him, "by my complexion."[18]

Cary's Liberian Mission

Cary stuck to his decision to leave the United States. In January 1821, fewer than eight years after purchasing his freedom, he led a group of twenty-eight free African American adults and an unknown number of children from Richmond for West Africa. This trip was not easy. It took forty-four grueling days to arrive in West Africa.[19] After the trip, it then took them roughly a year to purchase land from the locals to set up their community. During this time, they had to stay in Sierra Leone, where his second wife became ill and died, leaving him once again with two children to raise by himself.

After acquiring the land for the colony, Cary and the emigrants embarked for Liberia where they established a town they named *Monrovia*, after James Monroe, the president of the United States at that time. Monrovia was located along a stretch of coastline "between the Junk and Sesters Rivers and extending nearly seventy miles into the interior."[20]

The new emigrants faced many challenges, not only from the conditions but also from slave captors seeking slaves to sell. When Cary left Richmond, he probably did not think that he might end up captured and enslaved in Africa. But in Liberia, this was now a real possibility. To combat those challenges, the community erected fortifications to protect their members. In this way, the community resembled more of a military post than a mission during this early period.

Only one year after their arrival, more than one thousand Africans attacked Monrovia in an attempt to destroy it and capture its residents to sell to the slave trade. Although the United States had banned the international slave trade in 1808, some African slaves were still illegally transported into several Southern states. Had Cary or the others been captured, the emigrants could have ironically ended up back in America as slaves.

In the absence of anyone with a military background, Cary assumed the role of the colony's de facto military commander. Eventually Cary and a group of men, certainly numbering fewer than half of the invaders, repelled the invasion. After the battle, Cary sat down to write a letter to ACS supporters in America. Tired but relieved that they were not captured, Cary found strength and inspiration in the Bible. He compared the battle he had just led to the experience of the Jewish remnant in Jerusalem following their return from Babylonian exile, as recorded in Nehemiah 4:17: "the Jews, who, in rebuilding their city, 'grasped a weapon in one hand, while they labored with the other.'"[21]

Cary's dedication to his faith and the Liberian mission gave him the strength to continue. "There never has been an hour or a minute," Cary noted, "no, not even when the balls [gunfire] were flying around my head, when I could wish myself again in America."[22] Soon Cary would establish a Sunday school and a day school for locals from the surrounding areas, as gradually the military outpost began to look more like a mission.

Not only did Cary and other members of the colony have to fear locals, but they also suffered from a lack of funds. In 1823, Cary reached out to William Crane to ask for help. Cary's letters to Crane transcended racial divisions, and he spoke to Crane not as someone who saw himself as an inferior but as an equal— perhaps a friend. He opened the letter with the salutation "Dear brother." Cary continued by asking Crane and the members of the American Colonization Society to "lose no time in getting books sent on for this object, for that is the largest field for labor on this part of the coast."[23]

In another letter to Crane, Cary shared his feelings about slavery and the slave trade as he discussed the colony's battles against slave traders. But in this letter, Cary took the time to ensure that Crane would understand that the battle against slave traders was not just about the mission's safety, but also about their desire to fight against and liberate African captives from the slave traders. These liberated West Africans, according to Cary, "added greatly to our strength."[24]

For a former slave whose ancestors had been captured on the same shores where he now lived, it must have pleased Cary that the Liberian mission was saving other Africans from the horrors that his ancestors suffered during the Middle Passage. One wonders how Crane, a white man who seemed to view Cary as a friend and brother in the Lord, felt about the challenges that Cary and the colonists in Liberia faced.

By 1828, Cary's correspondence with the ACS reveals that Monrovia was making substantial progress. The missionary work, too, was moving forward.

> We have very few meetings but that some of the native-born sons of Ham are present, and they begin to learn to read and sing the praises of God. I should think that among your large population of colored people, if the love of themselves did not bring them out, the love of God would, for here is a wide and extensive missionary field.[25]

The Last Battle

In 1826, as a result of his hard work and dedication to the Liberian mission, Cary was elected vice agent of the colony. Two years later, he was promoted to the lead agent, basically making him the governor of all Monrovia. Considering his skills and intellect, Cary was an excellent choice. However, a long administration was not to be.

Only a few months after ascending to the top position in the colony, Cary tried to defend the colony against another invasion of the slave traders. As he had done numerous times, he assumed the position of de facto military leader and called the other leaders of the colony to take up arms to protect them from invasion. According to one of his biographers, Cary "considered himself solemnly bound to assert the rights and defend the property of the colony." The colony needed firearms and bullets. Cary joined a group of men who made cartridges as ammunition for firearms. Sadly, the room exploded, probably from the mix of powder and cartridges, killing Cary and several other men.[26]

Lott Cary died before he could see his mission fulfilled. But his life is a shining example of the power of faith when people turn to it, particularly in times of transition. Instead of becoming disillusioned with his life as a slave or as a freed person in America, he found inspiration in the Bible. He continued pressing forward. And by the time of his death, his church had one hundred baptized members. He died a hero attempting to stop slave traders from capturing potential slaves.

Colin Teague, another friend from Richmond who had originally traveled to Liberia with Cary and who had spent the last few years in Sierra Leone, returned to Liberia to help and defend the colony that his friend died for. Even in the wake of the period's greatest missionary in that section of Africa's demise, God continued to protect the people. Monrovia was a rock where the gospel of Jesus Christ continued to expand.

African American Lamentations: The Period of Abolitionism

As Black Americans entered the 1820s, many of them believed that America was in trouble unless the nation made a number of moral and ethical changes. The primary sources that Black people left behind during this period reveal their unshakable belief that God's judgment would bring America to its knees. In a sense, this perspective reflected an old prophetic tradition expressed by Old Testament prophets.

These men and women also wanted to return America to the promise and hopes of founders at the time of the American Revolution. In this sense, they were truly sons and daughters of the American Revolution.

David Walker was an advocate of this prophetic line of thought. Walker was born in North Carolina to a free mother and slave father. The fact that his mother was free ensured that he would be a free person. An African American's status was determined by the status of the mother.

Walker eventually moved to South Carolina and became active in the AME Church in Charleston. There he attended church with Denmark Vesey, a Black man who would later be executed for planning a rebellion against South Carolina in 1822. We do not know whether or not Walker was involved in that plot. We do know that shortly thereafter David left Charleston for Boston and quickly established himself as part of the city's prominent Black community.

Walker worked as a tailor and apparently did fairly well. He purchased a home that became a hub for abolitionists to gather. He also helped found the Massachusetts General Colored Association. The association was one of the first in America to specifically fight for the immediate end to slavery. Among these activists who would become involved in his circle were Maria Stewart and her husband, James. James Stewart was a prominent sailor and a wealthy businessman.

As an agent and writer for the *Freedom's Journal*, the first African American newspaper in the United States, Walker recognized his connections with sailors like Stewart would prove to be important. Although the newspaper and his connections to Boston's abolitionist community had done much to unite that community, Walker, who had lived in North Carolina and South Carolina, desperately wanted to speak to an even larger community. He wanted to bring Black people together across the entire Atlantic world.

To this end, in 1829, Walker published the *Appeal*, a work that largely established his legacy. Walker's *Appeal* was his dramatic plea for America to change and a call to free will. If individuals and America refused to do so, Walker believed that God's judgment would fall on them. Through the connections he made with local sailors, Walker was able to provide copies of the *Appeal* to these men, who then transported his writing throughout the Atlantic coast. Even today, this publication is difficult for us to categorize. On one hand, Walker was one of the most persuasive abolitionists, whose prophetic voice still encourages us to recognize the negative impact slavery had on Black people. However, for Walker, oppression did not mean that Black people could not respond.

Walker wrote, "God has been pleased to give us two eyes, two hands, two feet, and some sense in our heads as well as they." To Walker, Black people had to fight for their rights and take the first steps to liberate themselves.[27] "Let the aim of your labors among your brethren, and particularly the youths, be the dissemination of education and religion."[28] Walker had overcome much in his life and he wanted to inspire other African Americans to action. And this quote sums up Walker's argument that Black people, regardless of the degree of racial oppression, should not see slavery as reason not to pursue dreams, whether spiritual, educational, economic, or moral.

Walker's *Appeal* is neither a liberal nor conservative document but is better seen as a Christian treatise on life. The document has as much power today as it did in 1829. No matter our condition, Walker's underlying message is that we can all be agents of our destinies.

Sadly, Walker died less than a year after his appeal. Some historians believe that he was murdered. His words and his unshakable faith inspired those who met him and followed in the path he pursued.

Maria Stewart: A Servant of the Lord

Maria Stewart was one of the many people inspired by Walker's life and the ideas that he explored in his appeal. Born in Hartford, Connecticut, in 1803, Maria had a difficult childhood. We know nothing about her parents, as she was an orphan by the time she was five. From that age until about fifteen, she was bound out as a servant by the local court to a white clergyman's home. Maria received very little formal education, even though she did attend church schools at times.

From the age of fifteen, she started working as a domestic servant in other people's homes before marrying a free Black man named James Stewart when she was about nineteen. Stewart was a sailor, a veteran of the War of 1812, who by the time of their meeting was a successful businessman. As a man involved in maritime trade, life in a port city like Boston provided opportunities, even for a few Black people like Stewart.

The Stewarts became part of Boston's elite Black community that by this time included David Walker. The Stewarts and the Walkers were close. It is not difficult to imagine the families socializing at Walker's house discussing slavery and abolition. Perhaps they gathered for barbecues at each other's homes. At these gatherings, it is likely that Maria Stewart's opinions influenced David Walker and vice versa.

James Stewart died in 1829. Although he left Maria a sizeable estate, she was defrauded out of this. First, Maria Stewart should have received her husband's military pension at his death, which she was unable to acquire. Moreover, the white executors of his estate claimed the entire estate, leaving her without anything. Without money, Stewart had to return to the domestic work that she hated so much in order to pay her bills. Even though Stewart had never been a slave during her life, her life as a domestic led her to draw parallels between slavery and the work she did. It is from this experience that Stewart would later state:

> And such is the horrible idea that I entertain respecting a life of servitude, that if I conceived of there being no possibility of my rising above the condition of servant, I would gladly hail death as a welcome messenger. O, horrible idea, indeed to possess noble souls, aspiring after high and honorable acquirements, yet confined by the chains of ignorance and poverty to lives of continual drudgery and toil.[29]

Forced into domestic service again and deprived of the life that she had once enjoyed must have led Stewart to a dark place. The next year, Stewart experienced another traumatic loss as she learned of the death of David Walker—her friend and mentor. The two most influential men in her life died within a year. This period marked a turning point in her faith journey. Although she was a woman of faith throughout her life, she wrote that in 1830, at the height of her difficult times, she had a born-again experience and "made a public profession of my faith in Christ."[30]

Stewart's revival of faith led her to speak on the issues that plagued her community, and she dedicated her life to helping those who were less fortunate. As David Walker's life had demonstrated, the work of an abolitionist did not come without the threat of violence. But as someone who had already lost everything, she did not fear death: "I am firmly persuaded, that the God in whom I trust is able to protect me from the rage and malice of mine enemies."[31] She was so convinced of her calling that she was *willing* to die for it: "If there is no other way for me to escape, he is able to take me to himself, as he did the most noble, fearless, and undaunted David Walker."[32]

With her unshakable faith and desire to continue the legacy of her friend David Walker, Stewart began to write down her reflections. These writings served as a therapy of sorts, to express her innermost thoughts on race relations as well as her work to intervene in the struggle for rights. Writing also allowed her to talk about the prejudice she faced in her own life. She decided to send some of her writings to William Lloyd Garrison, the editor and founder of *The Liberator*, the most important abolitionist newspaper in America.

Garrison was also the founder of the American Anti-Slavery Society, the most prominent abolitionist society up until the Civil War. Stewart's excellent writing impressed Garrison, and he decided to publish some of her pieces in his newspaper. By

1832, Stewart was publicly speaking on abolitionist and women's issues, becoming one of the first women, if not the first, to speak publicly in America to mixed audiences of Black and white, male and female listeners.

Working with the American Anti-Slavery Society, her public life on the speaking circuit lasted roughly a year, and she retired from public speaking in 1833. Maria Stewart never relinquished her social engagement, however. By the end of her life in 1879, she had engaged in many leadership positions, including being a teacher, a founder of a Sunday school, and a matron of the Freedmen's Hospital (now Howard University Hospital) in Washington, DC.

Finding Empowerment in Service

Maria Stewart's ideologies, just like David Walker's, could not be restricted to our narrowly defined political spheres today. She was a sharp critic of slavery who advocated abolitionism in the strongest terms possible. At the same time, she argued that Black people had a responsibility to pursue morality. While other abolitionists tended to blame slavery and society as the reasons for immorality in their communities, Stewart always placed responsibility on the individual. We should see this stance as Stewart's way of forcefully arguing that Black people had power over their bodies and lives, which, for a slave or servant, undercut their "master's" authority. This was, indeed, a radical viewpoint.

While recognizing that her lack of opportunities may have limited her somewhat, she refused to use it as an excuse. "I possess nothing but moral capability—no teaching but the teaching of the Holy Spirit,"[33] Stewart said. To believe that Black people had power reflected her belief in free will. Even though Stewart realized the difficulties that Black people faced, she always believed that God provided opportunity. Thinking back to her lack of formal education she stated, "Had I received the advantages of early education, my ideas would, ere now, have expanded far and wide."[34] Yet Stewart never allowed life's struggles to extinguish her hope.

Maria Stewart, a woman who was born with so little, who gained prominence and status as a young woman only to lose it all as a young widow, is an example of the power of persistence. She recognized that God does not always provide social and economic wealth. Nonetheless, she believed that, as much as possible, everyone has a responsibility to live in the light of God regardless of his or her status. The apostle John wrote, "But if we walk in the light, as he is in the light, we have fellowship with one another, and the blood of Jesus, his Son, purifies us from all sin" (1 John 1:7).

In 1833, Stewart was asked to speak at the African Masonic Lodge in Boston. At the lodge, she told the people in the audience, "We have made ourselves appear altogether unqualified to speak in our own defense, and are therefore looked upon as objects of pity and commiseration." Unlike some abolitionists that viewed slaves as so destroyed by slavery they basically needed rehabilitation; Stewart focused on their intellectual progress. Stewart was not criticizing Black people who did not have education, but she wanted to encourage them to not use racism as reason for complacency.

What is remarkable about this speech is that she gave it while

> **BUT IF WE WALK IN THE LIGHT, AS HE IS IN THE LIGHT, WE HAVE FELLOWSHIP WITH ONE ANOTHER, AND THE BLOOD OF JESUS, HIS SON, PURIFIES US FROM ALL SIN. (1 JOHN 1:7)**

speaking to a group of Black men. As one of the first women to stand in front of men and speak, Stewart did not hold back. "Talk, without effort, is nothing; you are abundantly capable, gentlemen, of making yourselves men of distinction; and this gross neglect, on your part, causes my blood to boil within me." She continued, "Here is the grand cause which hinders the rise and progress of the people of color. It is their want of laudable ambition and requisite courage." While much of this is hyperbole, Stewart wanted Black men to be strong in the face of oppression. And she would stand with them.[35]

Stewart's views on community responsibility place her in the Black nationalist camp with David Walker, although she was careful not to advocate violence to accomplish her goals. She stated: "African rights and liberty is a subject that ought to fire the breast of every free man of color in these United States, and excite in his bosom a lively, deep, decided and heart-felt interest."[36] As Black people came together, Stewart believed they would recognize that their condition would be poor "unless by true piety and virtue, we strive to regain that which we have lost."[37]

Stewart's interests extended beyond slavery. She supported temperance and increasing access to education for everyone.

She said, "You have been told repeatedly of the glorious results arising from temperance, and can you bear to see the whites arising in honor and respectability, without endeavoring to grasp after that honor and respectability also?" She charged Black people to be "promoters of temperance, and the supporters, as far as we are able, of useful and scientific knowledge."[38] In this way, Stewart reflected the ideas of other postmillennialists who wanted to prepare the nation for the millennium. To this end, she encouraged Black people in addition to pushing for abolition to form educational and temperance societies.

At the same time, Stewart believed that white people had responsibility to atone for their sins in regard to racism. Just as David Walker did, she criticized the ACS saying, "If they (ACS) are real friends to Africa, let them expend the money which they collect, in erecting a college to educate her injured sons." She later stated that white peoples' "hearts are so frozen towards us, they had rather their money should be sunk in the ocean than to administer it to relief; and I fear, if they dared, like Pharaoh, king of Egypt, they would order every male child among us to be drowned."[39]

In the end, Stewart believed in God's providence and that He would raise up leaders if people were willing to be used by God:

> But many powerful sons and daughters of Africa will shortly arise, who will put down vice and immorality among us, and declare by Him that sitteth upon the throne, that they will have their rights; and if refused, I am afraid they would spread horror and devastation around.[40]

This fit into Stewart's view of the end times, that Black people need only to awake and "save our sons from dissipation, and our daughters from ruin."[41] When Black people did so, she believed that they would usher in a new society. She said, "I believe that the oppression of injured Africa has come up before the Majesty of Heaven; and when our cries shall have reached the ears of the Most High, it will be a tremendous day for the people of this land; for strong is the arm of the Lord God Almighty."[42]

Stewart was unshakable in her belief that Black people could win the struggle for racial justice as long as they let God lead them.[43]

Black Women in the Struggle

While David Walker rarely spoke in his *Appeal* about the important role of women in the freedom struggle, women's rights were important to Maria Stewart. As a Black woman who realized the intersectionality of her status as a Black person and Black woman in society, she felt prejudice on account of her race and gender. And yet Stewart sometimes pleaded with Black men not only to respect her as a woman but also to take a larger role in the freedom struggle: "I would ask, is it blindness of mind, or stupidity of soul, or the want of education, that has caused our men who are sixty or seventy years of age never to let their voices be heard nor their hands be raised in behalf of their color?"[44]

Even though Stewart wanted men to be part of the struggle and, perhaps, even lead it, she could not envision a world where women were subservient. She was adamant that Black men and women work together. As a woman whose hands had folded and washed clothes and toiled as a servant in others' homes, she was not going to tell women to be *less* than men. She knew how that felt. What she wanted was equality—but one where men were responsible to women. In some ways, she transcended the cult of domesticity, however, by expecting that men and women live up to the same standards.[45]

As Scripture says, she exhorted them, "Come, let us turn unto the Lord our God, with all our heart and soul, and put away every unclean and unholy thing from among us, and walk before the Lord our God, with a perfect heart, all the days of our lives."[46] Indeed, according to Maria, these biblical principles of temperance, intelligence, and moral fortitude were for all people, regardless of their gender.[47]

Women, according to Stewart, needed to exert their power in order to fulfill their destinies. Stewart believed that God worked through women and instilled in them the strength to overcome. And she believed God provided an avenue to victory regardless of whether a man was there for them or not. She knew that Jesus makes us conquerors of life "through him who hath loved [us] and given himself for [us]."[48]

As we look at the life of Maria Stewart, we should remember how much we need to lift each other up, regardless of who we are. She wanted justice, but she first sought out the Lord. In doing so, Maria Stewart's words then and now inspire and empower people from all backgrounds. To Stewart, as Paul attested, Christ is the foundation of true freedom and a moral life (see 1 Thessalonians 4:1).

Explore Your Faith with Lott Cary and Maria Stewart

* How can we use Lott Cary's exemplary life to help us overcome divisions?

* What does it mean for us that God took Cary from a slave to manager and eventually to governor of a colony?

* How did faith bring Lott Cary and William Crane together? What message does that have for people today?

* Maria Stewart saw a place for men and women as co-equals. How successful are our churches in hearing her call some two hundred years later?

* Maria Stewart believed that we should encourage each other. How are we doing this, and how do we do so better?

CHAPTER 3

JOURNEY TO CANAAN: FREEDOM AND INDEPENDENCE

The Lord had said to Abram, "Go from your country, your people and your father's household to the land I will show you. I will make you into a great nation, and I will bless you; I will make your name great, and you will be a blessing. I will bless those who bless you, and whoever curses you I will curse; and all peoples on earth will be blessed through you."

GENESIS 12:1–3

God's call to Abram, whom God turned into *Abraham*, is one of the seminal moments in human history. When God called Abram and his family, they became the first example of a biblical conversion. Abram and his family gave up their previous ways and beliefs to embark on a journey leading them to a personal relationship with God. God not only called them to a greater understanding of Him, but through them, He also prepared an entire nation to accept their call to greatness. God's promise to Abraham did not end there. Today all Christians share in God's new covenant through Jesus Christ. Indeed, God's commitment to us still reigns today!

The book of Exodus features the rescue of the Israelites from Egypt and their constitution as a nation set aside for God's purposes in the world. The book of Exodus is much more, however. In it, we see that slavery and oppression had psychological consequences on the oppressed. We see God working with His people throughout the book of Exodus to free them not only physically but also psychologically.

The Bible reveals to us that the Israelites were in Egypt for 430 years. Over that period, they witnessed their status decline into slavery. Throughout, God never forgot His covenant with them. Indeed, He raised up Moses to lead them out of Egypt and fulfilled His promise to Abraham. God said: "See, I have given you this land. Go in and take possession of the land the LORD swore he would give to your fathers—to Abraham, Isaac and Jacob—and to their descendants after them" (Deuteronomy 1:8).

The experience of slavery and the exodus out of it helped shape the worldview of the Israelites. For instance, when God gave Moses the Ten Commandments on Mount Sinai, He reminded the Israelites of their enslavement and of the fact He expected them to use the experience to make themselves a better people: "I am the LORD your God, who brought you out of Egypt, out of the land of slavery" (Exodus 20:2). In the book of Leviticus, we see God again imploring the Israelites to use the exodus experience as a model for the kind of society they would build: "The foreigner residing among you must be treated as your native-born. Love them as yourself, for you were foreigners in Egypt. I am the LORD your God" (Leviticus 19:34).

God wanted the Israelites to remember their captivity in Egypt as a defining moment in their existence. This is a message that transcends time. Today, the meaning is just as clear and important. Simply stated, when we come out of a storm, God wants us to reflect on the experience and to grow from it.

The exodus has a special place in the African American experience. African American slaves treasured the story even though slave masters certainly did not want them to focus on God liberating slaves. Slaves found comfort in knowing that God always cares for the oppressed and that He is preparing a way for their liberation.

The story of the exodus also reveals that freedom is not an end to life's challenges but a beginning to new ones. When we move from one situation to another, these transitions can be difficult, even for the saints of God. Life's transitions can be extremely taxing. Indeed, crossing from slavery into freedom is something particularly challenging. The Israelites' experiences detailed in the exodus reveal just how challenging.

In Exodus 14:12, the Israelites asked Moses if it were not better for them to remain in Egypt than to die in the wilderness. Simply stated, the Israelites had been so psychologically affected by their mistreatment that they felt they needed the Egyptians to survive. Perhaps, today, we may call it *post-traumatic stress disorder (PTSD)* or a version of Stockholm syndrome. The Israelites' oppression scared them in ways that led them to second-guess themselves. Such anxiety is entirely normal. Perhaps, they felt *impostor syndrome,* the persistent sense of doubt about one's true skills and abilities and fear of being evaluated as inadequate. As American slaves moved from slavery to freedom, they felt this way too. Even today, people can feel this way after an abusive relationship of one sort or another, or when someone loses their job or is fired, for example.

Moses understood all of these fears, and encouraged the Israelites. As he stood on the banks of the Red Sea, Moses implored: "Do not be afraid. Stand firm and you will see the deliverance the LORD will bring you today. The Egyptians you see today you will never see again" (Exodus 14:13). As children of God we, too, should hold on to these words when we feel anxiety or depression caused by something or someone from our past.

The Promised Land

By the 1850s, most African Americans had been introduced to the Christian faith. As the nation was on the brink of war, Black religious believers were remarkably united. As we saw in the previous chapters, the Christian faith helped unite Black people as numerous AME, AME Zion, Baptist, Presbyterian, and Episcopalian churches provided a place of sanctuary from slavery and racism for African Americans. The church's dedication to spiritual formation and moral guidance provided tremendous support for their lives. Black people preferred African American houses of worship, but not because they did not want to worship with white parishioners. Their preference resulted from the fact that integrated worship settings typically relegated Black people to the background.

Black people wanted the opportunity to practice their faith in an affirming environment. They listened to Black ministers and the Black deacon boards that checked in on them. In many African American churches, deacon boards also served as judicial councils and were the only places where church members could seek nonracist justice. In a society where justice was basically nonexistent, these councils that dispensed justice and mediated disputes between members offered the most likely form of adjudication possible.

At the same time, many churches since the Second Great Awakening had fractured. As Black Churches grew their memberships, white denominations divided during the antebellum period. Nowhere was this more apparent than in the church of the post-1840s. Although it is historically inaccurate to say that the divisions among believers led to the Civil War, it's certainly true that the form of racism and slavery that emerged in the antebellum period and the prejudice that surrounded it hurt the unity of churches as well as our nation.

For a moment, let us consider the effects of racism and slavery on the antebellum church, existing during the twenty-year period before the Civil War. Slavery divided both the Northern and Southern Baptist and Methodist denominations into separate factions in the 1840s. Later, the Presbyterian Church separated over slavery into two factions, although divisions in this church had existed since at least the 1830s.

It is important to state this: The foundations of American Christianity for all Americans remained the same. However, Black Churches and some white churches in the North applied the gospel in ways that directly confronted slavery and racism. Preaching the social gospel with the tenets of the faith was a unifying thing. The Black Church in both the North and the South centered on the liberation of Black people, while, at the same time, maintaining a fairly conservative Christian theology.

While we would prefer that Southern white ministers and more in the North had challenged slavery more directly during the antebellum period, it's important to realize that a few pushed beyond social conventions in order to stake out some ground toward a more equitable society.

Challenging laws and local customs by pushing the boundaries of acceptable behavior, antebellum ministers of the gospel such as Reverends Alexander Glennie and Charles Colcock Jones saw it as their duty to evangelize the slave population. Against South Carolina law, Glennie performed hundreds of slave marriages, and even carried a ring with him to commemorate the services he performed. On some occasions, he permitted slaves to conduct religious services as well as to read the liturgy and perform catechisms.[1]

Other white ministers worked within local customs and laws to provide some freedoms for African Americans. In these cases white ministers concluded that spreading God's Word was more important than state laws and customs that sought to restrict God's Word. When Robert Ryland, president of Virginia

Baptist Seminary (today's *University of Richmond*), accepted the call to become pastor of the First African Baptist Church in Richmond, he probably did not know how his religious beliefs led him to quietly defy local custom. Although Ryland publicly supported slavery, he had some misgivings about the institution. Ryland believed that African Americans had the intelligence and the necessary skills to successfully serve as church leaders. He distributed religious literature to church members and opened a library at the church.

When Ryland wrote the first history of the church years later, he recalled the church leaders were "an intelligent, godly, and highly respected body of men." By being a hands-off leader in this situation, Ryland afforded African American leaders an opportunity to define the direction they felt God was leading them.[2]

In granting these privileges to his congregation, Ryland came very close to violating Virginia law—and even went beyond that law on occasion. In particular, he encouraged the members of his church to read. Ryland was unrepentant in his feelings that the state was wrong to restrict the ability to teach African Americans to read and write, stating, "the prohibition to teach colored children to read the Word of God, except under very limited conditions . . . glaring wrongs." The restrictions against Black preachers were another area where Ryland pushed against Virginia law. Although Ryland did not formally allow Black men to preach from the pulpit, as this was illegal, he gave them the opportunity to engage the church in extended prayer from the floor. He clearly intended that these prayers be, in effect, illegal sermons. He also encouraged his ministers to pray in the same manner at Black funerals.[3]

The fact that some white and Black believers in the South continued working together even during the antebellum period is an important message for believers today. Today it often appears that our society is too fractured for people from different perspectives to work together for positive change. Collaboration is always possible when both sides see the Christian body as a place for transformation and growth. When we draw nearer to Jesus and open ourselves to His guidance, He draws us closer to our brothers and sisters.

Ryland recognized how important community was to the church leaders he worked with daily. Ryland reported that "in all their convocations, they, each and every one, had not only their own spiritual culture, [but also] the salvation of their people, the peace and order of society, and the glory of God." Indeed, Ryland realized just how powerful the Black Church was. Its impact was tremendous. Church leaders understood that uplifting their race through the church could boost them individually too. As a community that opened its doors both to slave and free African Americans, the church was a source of pride as well as an institution to pursue larger moral and intellectual goals.[4]

As the Black Church developed during the antebellum period, however, we must recognize that any church is a group of believers. It was not the Black Church per se that was the center of social life. The church isn't merely a building. Buildings without engaged believers cannot have any positive spiritual impact. What made the Black Church important was the faith of individuals that united to make it the center of Black social life.

As the 1850s turned into the 1860s, faith continued to sustain Black people. It was this faith that put them on a firm foundation as they emerged from the war as free people. Real faith empowered them to embark on a journey of discovery for themselves, their communities, and their nation.

Booker and Harriet

When we think about historical persons to link together, few people would consider Harriet Tubman and Booker T. Washington. Today Harriet Tubman is universally lauded as one of the most important Black leaders ever. While she was certainly recognized in the late nineteenth and early twentieth centuries, her stature has increased today. In 2019, the movie *Harriet* brought her story to millions of viewers. During the same time, Booker T. Washington's stature has diminished significantly. This is a far cry from 1915 when he died as the most recognized African American leader in the world.

Faith and slavery were perhaps the two strongest themes throughout their lives. Both were scarred by their experiences of slavery. But their faith provided them the help they needed, as well as the necessary encouragement, to conquer their fears. As time passed and they each gained freedom, God opened up leadership roles for both. Neither Tubman nor Washington forgot their humble experiences while enslaved, and they used these experiences as their incentive to help others.

Today it is easy to exaggerate the differences between Tubman and Washington, particularly considering our modern-day obsession with categorizing people according to our interpretation of being "woke." In evaluating people of the past, we must recognize the obstacles and the times they lived in. We should not put our own conventions on people like Booker T. Washington. While it may seem more politically woke to celebrate Tubman's active radicalism as compared to Washington's perceived conservatism, this conclusion is shortsighted. Furthermore, sometimes it is easy to dismiss the central role that Tubman's faith played in her radicalism. Similarly, we may forget the many ways that Washington quietly challenged and radically pushed against racism and discrimination.

Harriet Tubman: The Moses of Her People

"Go Down Moses" is one of the most known African American spirituals. The song reminds us that God loves us and that He is constantly stepping in to lead us to spiritual and physical liberation.

Harriet Tubman, the African American hero most identified with the biblical Moses, also knew and sang a version of this song. Indeed, it is not surprising that Tubman found hope in the power of its inspiring lyrics. The story of Moses and the exodus has tremendous similarities to the African American experience. African American slaves recognized that the Israelites, too, were enslaved.

Perhaps Tubman and the slaves who sang "Go Down Moses" saw themselves as the embodiment of the Israelites. Just as Moses and the Israelites had to overcome their psychological and mental barriers to accept the liberation that God had prepared for them, African American slaves recognized that, in order for them to be truly free, they also had to step forward and trust that God was leading them to freedom.

Additionally, African Americans understood that the story of the exodus demonstrates that faith is the foundation to action. In order to realize God's plan, the Israelites had to step out on faith. And so did Harriet.[5]

Like many Christian slaves and free people, Harriet held close to a personal God who was active in the lives of believers. She believed that God was omnipresent and that He was capable of doing everything that He did in the Old Testament.

Tubman was illiterate and, because of this, expressed her messages not through her writings but by reciting Black spirituals. She sang these spirituals as a testimony of her faith. They spoke of her understanding of biblical history while affirming her belief that Jesus Christ is the same yesterday, today, and forever.

When Tubman traveled through Maryland, setting up communication lines with slaves to help them escape captivity, she used the spiritual "Go Down Moses" to communicate with them. Tubman stated that if she sang the following verse, it was unsafe for them to come out:

> Moses go down in Egypt,
> Till ole Pharos' let me go;
> Hadn't been for Adam's fall,
> Shouldn't hab to died at all[6]

Even if the message was that the path was not yet clear, her words still provided hope to the slaves. They could take comfort that Tubman would remain in touch with them until the path was clear for their escape. Tubman's faith was a lived faith, with a deep personal belief in, and relationship with, the Lord.

It inspired her through her tough years in captivity and led to her decision to risk her freedom for the liberation of her people. Just like Moses, Tubman believed in the power of God to do the miraculous as she stepped out in faith.

Tubman's faith was an applied faith. She conditioned her mind to believe that she would be successful by taking inspiration from truth, the biblical stories. Today's Christians could strive to emulate Tubman's belief and application of that faith to Christian ministry.

Faith in Captivity

Born a slave around 1820 on the Eastern Shore of Maryland, Harriet Tubman (at birth named Araminta Ross) had a difficult life. As a resident of Maryland, Tubman lived in a state that by 1850 had roughly the same percentage of slaves as it did free African Americans. Therefore, she grasped the differences between African American slavery and freedom. As a young woman, she met and interacted with many free African Americans. Even though the lives of free African Americans were not easy, they had rights she did not have. When she married a free African American man, she quickly came to realize that he legally could not be sold while she and all their children could be.

Tubman's early years were filled with uncertainty and hardship. Throughout these difficult experiences, Tubman relied on the Lord. Tubman's master often hired her out. Although some other examples of hiring out in this book were somewhat positive for the slave, in Tubman's case this was not true. One of the women that Tubman was hired to Tubman referred to simply as *Susan*. Susan was a woman filled with hate, and she was emotionally and physically abusive to Tubman. In describing one of the incidents of abuse, Tubman stated to her biographer:

> She drew her up to the table, saying, "What do you mean by doing my work this way, you—!" And passing her finger on the table and piano, she showed her the mark it made through the dust. "Miss Susan, I have swept and dusted just as you told me." But the whip was already taken down, and the strokes were falling on head and face and neck.[7]

The cycle of abuse was a consistent element throughout Tubman's years as a slave. After the prior experience of abuse, her master hired Harriet to another person, and the abuse became worse. One day the man threw a scale that hit Tubman on her head, causing permanent damage. Because of the injury, Tubman suffered from blackouts and dizziness for the remainder of her life.

When Tubman returned to her owner around 1850, one might think that he would have attended to her because of the abuse she had sustained. However, he immediately made plans to sell her because he considered her to be troublesome. As a slave living in Maryland, Tubman realized that many slaves were being sold further south to the flourishing cotton and rice plantations of the lower and Gulf South. Tubman knew that if she were sold she would never see her family and husband again.

In this dark time, Tubman reached out to God. She also reached out to her master hoping that by working as hard as she could that her master would reconsider selling her:

> From Christmas until March I worked as
> I could, and I prayed all the long nights—I
> groaned and prayed for old master; Oh Lord,
> convert master! Oh Lord, change that man's
> heart.[8]

Yet fearing her immediate sale, Tubman still found the strength to forgive him. Instead of hating the people who abused and mistreated her—she prayed for their salvation.

Preparing for what she believed to be her sale further south, Tubman not only prayed for her master's salvation, but she also asked the Lord to cleanse her of her sin: "Wash me, make me clean . . . Oh, Lord wipe away all my sin . . . Oh Lord, whatsoever sin there be in my heart, sweep it out."[9]

Through prayer, Tubman realized that God wanted her to be free and that, just as He did with the Israelites, He was preparing her for that freedom. No matter what her master wanted, Tubman was now convinced that God wanted her to escape from captivity. When recalling her escape from slavery, she recited another spiritual called "When the Chariot Comes," which she used to convey to others her plans to escape.

> I'm gonna be, got to be ready
> When the chariot comes
> I'm gonna be, got to be ready
> When the chariot comes
> When the chariot comes

Tubman understood the song's double meaning. The chariot was a symbol of her opportunity to be free: a freedom God himself was preparing her for. But, at the same time, Tubman understood that "When the Chariot Comes" had a deeper meaning. It conveyed her belief in the second coming of Jesus Christ. Thus, the song represented Tubman's own belief in the historical reality of the Bible, its application to her life, and the truth, as found in God's Word, regarding the end times.

Finding Freedom and Her Voice

When we submit to God, we take the first step to freedom. Throughout history, we have seen blessings that come to those who humble themselves to God. Harriet Tubman is but one example. Tubman submitted to God and, in doing so, found the strength to escape from her master. When Tubman escaped, she didn't even know the path she was taking. She trusted in the Lord. Not knowing the way to freedom, Tubman thought back to the stories from the Bible to inspire her.

God led her through the forests, away from dogs searching for escaped slaves, and to safe houses where she could stay and rest on her journey. Along the way, she found encouragement in the exodus. It gave her proof that God is able to lead people to freedom even if they do not know the direction they are traveling.

Thomas Garrett, a friend of Tubman's, recognized the impact of Tubman's faith on her life, and how it guided her to freedom. Garrett stated that when she went into territory to rescue slaves, she listened to the voice of God. She "ventured only where God sent her, and her faith in a superior power truly was great."[10]

When Tubman reached freedom in Philadelphia, she knew that her mission had only begun. She praised God for liberating her and believed that if she continued to pray that He would give her the strength to carry on. Now a free woman, Tubman focused on another one of the central lessons she took from the exodus: never forget that God not only wants us to be free. He wants us to remember our exodus as a foundation to do good for others.

Tubman had family members and friends who were still enslaved. Should she try to liberate them, or should she leave them enslaved? For Tubman, the answer was easy. She had learned from the exodus that she should not forget her family or her experiences in slavery. With this in mind, Tubman decided to risk her own hard-fought freedom, and made the commitment to liberate others.

"There are two things I've got a right to, and these are, Death or Liberty—one or the other I mean to have," Tubman stated. "No one will take me back alive; I shall fight for my liberty, and when the time has come for me to go, the Lord will let them, kill me."[11]

This spirit gave Tubman the power to lead at least twenty expeditions in slave territory to liberate other slaves, including her family members. Even though "dead-or-alive" rewards were placed against Tubman, God kept Harriet safe through all her travels back South to liberate other African Americans.[12] God responded to Tubman's obedience.

He protected her on her new mission. God led her through the Civil War as she became a nurse and spy, a hero serving her nation. Tubman used her knowledge of the trails and pathways in the South to travel into territory often reserved for men. Even after the war, Tubman continued to advocate for people.

She supported giving the vote to women, and other aspects

> "THERE ARE TWO THINGS I'VE GOT A RIGHT TO, AND THESE ARE, DEATH OR LIBERTY—ONE OR THE OTHER I MEAN TO HAVE," TUBMAN STATED. "NO ONE WILL TAKE ME BACK ALIVE; I SHALL FIGHT FOR MY LIBERTY, AND WHEN THE TIME HAS COME FOR ME TO GO, THE LORD WILL LET THEM, KILL ME."

of women's rights. Living her last years in relative poverty, she worked tirelessly to support elderly African Americans through her work in the AME Zion Church, even donating some of her land to the endeavor. When she died in 1911, she was somewhere around ninety years of age.

Hearing and Responding to the Call

Sometimes we reject God's call because we do not think we are worthy of it, forgetting that if God calls us He will also equip us for His purpose. Although Tubman was illiterate, enslaved, and had seizures, God used her for His purpose. As we consider what might seem to be impossible, all we have to do is be reminded of Harriet Tubman and her faith. She was a believer in God and in the power of prayer. Through belief and prayer, God equips us.

One can imagine the descendants of slaves that Tubman liberated, who then forged ahead in freedom in their new lives. These experiences surely made Tubman grateful. Faith in God had made it all possible. God had equipped Harriet, who had unshakable faith.

King David, after hearing God's call, learned how God would equip him:

> Now I will make your name great, like the names of the greatest men on earth. And I will provide a place for my people Israel and will plant them so that they can have a home of their own and no longer be disturbed. (2 Samuel 7:8–10)

No matter what our circumstances, God delivers. If He could deliver Moses . . . King David . . . if He could deliver Harriet, God can certainly deliver us.

Booker T. Washington: A Complex Man

On September 18, 1895, Booker T. Washington stood on a podium to deliver a speech before an integrated audience at the Cotton States and International Exposition held in Atlanta, Georgia. The exposition was a large gathering of businesspersons who wanted to promote Southern businesses.

> NOW I WILL MAKE YOUR NAME GREAT, LIKE THE NAMES OF THE GREATEST MEN ON EARTH. AND I WILL PROVIDE A PLACE FOR MY PEOPLE ISRAEL AND WILL PLANT THEM SO THAT THEY CAN HAVE A HOME OF THEIR OWN AND NO LONGER BE DISTURBED. (2 SAMUEL 7:8–10)

While the exposition's trustees presented an image of a "New South" to the world, they were silent on the fact that while the South had improved economically, the conditions for African Americans had declined drastically since the end of Reconstruction in 1877.

During the speech, Washington expounded on the views that he had crafted over the previous fifteen years in his role as founder and principal of the Tuskegee Normal and Industrial Institute (referred to as *Tuskegee Institute* or *Tuskegee* in this chapter) in Alabama. His tenure at Tuskegee Institute crossed the era of Reconstruction, a period that commenced with tremendous promise for African Americans. But on that day in 1895, he stood speaking to white businessmen during the height of Jim Crow racism. He had no way of knowing whether any of the men in the audience had lynched a Black person. He did not even know if they wanted to charge the stage and lynch him. If they did, he knew that there was little chance to stop them and even less chance for any justice.

Between 1868 and 1875, Congress passed a series of laws expanding the rights of African Americans. By the early 1870s, African American leaders like Frederick Douglass believed that America might become a truly integrated nation. Over a period of a few years, African Americans rose from the shackles of slavery to the highest offices in the land. In 1875, Congress even passed a civil rights act to protect African Americans from violations of their legal and civil rights. The act also protected African Americans from being denied access to public accommodations.

This period of optimism did not last long. The return to power of the "Redeemers," a group of Southern leaders who introduced the historically inaccurate "lost-cause" narrative, made life difficult for African Americans. The lost-cause narrative, which erroneously presents the formation of the Confederacy in heroic terms and argued that slaves were satisfied with their status in the South, was launched in response to the positive changes for African Americans in the South during the latter parts of Reconstruction. Believing in this ideology, hate groups such as the Ku Klux Klan and the Knights of the White Camelia emerged. These organizations often resorted to violence to keep Black people from organizing politically or promoting their economic interests.

In 1883, the Supreme Court opened the doors to a further erosion of African Americans' rights, when in a series of decisions, it declared much of the Civil Rights Act of 1875 unconstitutional, particularly the parts of the act that outlawed discrimination by individuals. In the years after this decision, state legislatures pushed forward more aggressively toward total segregation, particularly in the South.

After Reconstruction, there were other transitions for African Americans. Only a few months before Washington's speech, Frederick Douglass, the most known Black leader in America, died. Douglass represented a generation of leaders who came to adulthood during slavery, and had led the African American community during the period of Reconstruction.

A few months after Douglass's death, the Supreme Court upheld the Louisiana Supreme Court's decision regarding Homer Plessy, an African American from Louisiana who had been arrested and convicted for sitting in a "whites-only" train car, and gave a green light to laws that segregated the races throughout the nation.

This is what made Washington's speech so important. He understood the progress Black people had made as well as the declines of the previous decade. Had something gone wrong it could have led to open season on all Black leaders. For that reason alone, he understood the moment in which he stood. The absence of civil equality demanded that Black leaders had to pursue different strategies than they did in the early Reconstruction period in order to push their agenda forward.

Booker T. Washington was a perfect man for this new period. Instead of speaking bluntly about the equality he desperately wanted, he appealed to moderate white Southerners by focusing on Black economics. Instead of talking about voting rights, Washington asked for a bargain between white businessmen and Black workers, one that on the surface appears more beneficial to those businessmen.

In return for employing Black workers, Washington expected Black people to forgive white people for slavery and to work with them. To both Black and white, he exhorted, "Cast down your bucket where you are—cast it down in making friends in every manly way of the people of all races by whom we are surrounded."[13] Washington understood that the bargain was unequal, but he also realized it was the best deal that African Americans could pursue at that time. Washington summed up his views of integration in this manner: "In all things that are purely social we can be as separate as the fingers, yet one as the hand in all things essential to mutual progress."[14]

Up from Slavery through Sunday School

Born a slave in 1856 in Virginia, Washington had few advantages of birth. Washington was the son of a slave mother and a white man. Washington's mother, Jane, worked as a cook for her master.

After Washington's birth, his mother married an African American man named Washington ("Wash") Ferguson. After the end of slavery, Wash Ferguson found work in the salt mines in West Virginia and sent for the rest of his family to join him. Ferguson was the dominant figure in the household, maybe abusive in a sense, who forced all his wife's children to work in the salt mines.[15]

Booker T. Washington's tough experiences in the salt mines made him a strong advocate of education. Salt mining is dangerous work. Working underground can lead to dehydration, and the work takes a heavy toll on a person's health. Lacking open space in the mines, the young Washington ingested high levels of salt that may have contributed to the hypertension that he suffered later in life.

Even though Washington wanted to go to school after he returned from the salt mines, his stepfather initially refused to allow him to do so. The only education the young Booker T. Washington had came at the Sunday school at the Baptist church in the town of Tinkersville. During Sunday school, Washington learned about the Lord. He soon made a profession of faith and was baptized. Washington remained a Baptist throughout his life.[16]

Sunday school had a particularly influential role throughout Washington's life. For Washington, the short lessons the teachers taught on Sunday morning opened a window into the world beyond the salt mines. The Sunday school also served as a class-room. There the instructors helped him learn to read and write. The classroom filled with interested young students only bol-stered his interest in education.

Recalling his first exposure to Sunday school, Washing-ton remembered being a poor young man struggling over the recent death of his mother, and from the abusive conditions in the mines, and feeling utterly hopeless. One of the leaders in the community invited him to Sunday school. "Sonny, I want you to go with me to Sunday-school," Washington remembered. Washington did not even know what Sunday school was, but the man "led me, a poor, unknown Negro boy, into the Sunday-school, and I have been interested in the Sunday-school ever since." [17] As in Washington's time, there is no hope in the solu-tions addressing the problems that confront us in the South aside from solutions based upon the teachings of the Bible. [18]

Inspired by what he was learning in church and Sunday school, Washington did not allow his experiences in the salt mines and with his stepfather to deter him from dreaming. And he found out that he was a quick learner. Wanting to learn more, he kept asking his stepfather to allow him to attend school. His persistence eventually paid off, and his stepfather agreed. The

> THERE IS NO HOPE IN THE SOLUTIONS ADDRESSING THE PROBLEMS THAT CONFRONT US IN THE SOUTH ASIDE FROM SOLUTIONS BASED UPON THE TEACHINGS OF THE BIBLE.

deal with his stepfather required Washington to work in the mines for five hours starting at four in the morning, to go to school afterward, and to return to the mines after school.

This had to have been hard. The effects of salt poisoning may have even caused him to go to school suffering from dizziness or fever.[19] In addition to the salt mines, Washington worked in dirty, polluted coal mines. These experiences brought hardships but also taught him the lessons he carried with him the remainder of his life.

Working in the mines one day, Washington heard other miners talking about a school named *Hampton* that would admit students like him. He wrote, "Although I had no idea where it was, or how many miles away, or how I was going to reach it; I remembered only that I was on fire constantly with one ambition, and that was to go to Hampton. This thought was with me day and night."[20]

Just as Harriet Tubman had, Washington felt that God wanted him to leave a place he knew well to pursue the destiny that God had prepared for him. In both cases, neither forgot the communities they came from.

Faith and Works in Action

Although our works do not redeem us, they are a sign of our obedience to God. Booker T. Washington's faith gave him strength and focus to do great works. At the forefront of his faith was his belief in the power of forgiveness. He also believed that his faith gave him the inspiration to seek self-sufficiency in his personal life while relying on God for spiritual matters. Washington saw the church as a liberating force. The church was the institution responsible for his early education, as was the case for many rural Black people of the time.

Washington's faith developed even more at Hampton Normal and Agricultural Institute (now Hampton University) where he found a faculty and staff invested in his development. In particular, Nathalie Lord, a white teacher whose lineage included Congregational missionaries, had a major role in his spiritual development. Lord took an interest in the young Washington when she arrived at Hampton during his second year. Lord's influence on Washington's life became strong. Recalling their interactions years later, he wrote:

> [She] taught me how to use and love the Bible. Before this I had never cared a great deal about it, but now I learned to love to read the Bible, not only for the spiritual help which it gives, but on account of it as literature. The lessons taught me in this respect took such a hold upon me that at the present time, when I am at home, no matter how busy I am, I make it a rule to read a chapter or portion of a chapter . . . before beginning the work of the day.[21]

As Lord encouraged Washington to read the Bible daily, Washington had an impact on Lord too. She invited Washington and two of his other classmates to study the Bible, and each day the four gathered to study and pray together. By the end of the year she recalled, "We had read together the Gospels, Acts and Epistles."[22]

Years later, after Washington had become the leader of the Tuskegee Institute, Lord recalled that young Washington had talked to her a lot about his family and friends back in West Virginia and that he prayed that they would one day enjoy the privileges he enjoyed. Lord and Washington prayed together for their lives to improve. No matter how much Washington wanted them to be able to come to Hampton, however, he was more interested in them living with faith and integrity.[23]

A Table in the Presence of My Enemies

One of the problems many people have with Booker T. Washington is his commitment to dialogue, even with people who were openly racist. Today we have words for handling discussions with people we disagree with: *canceling, pausing, unfriending,* and so on. It is easy to push to the margins (or out of our lives altogether) people we disagree with politically, denominationally, religiously. *Cancel culture,* as it is sometimes referred to, is a short-sighted way to address life in a diverse society. Our Christian faith, rather, encourages us to *welcome* those with whom we disagree. Our Great Commission is to go into the world and bring people to Christ (Matthew 28:19–20). Jesus did not cancel the woman at the well. Or Zacchaeus. Indeed, Jesus did not cancel Peter for denying him before He went to trials and the cross.

Cancel culture is often rooted in arrogance or our desire to protect our ideas and thoughts from any dissent. This does not mean that we have to agree with every other thought we encounter. But when we quickly cancel the thoughts of others, we are the ones beginning from a place of weakness. As Christians, we know the truth. We have already claimed the victory through

Christ. Jesus, our model, has demonstrated to us the reality that it is important to embrace others, especially as we should want to lead them to Christ.

When Booker T. Washington graduated from Hampton in 1875, Reconstruction was winding down. Washington understood that US society demanded a different kind of leader. The leaders of this era could not push a radical agenda, or even one that advanced civil rights. Instead, they would use the language that Southern white men and women could understand.

Several years after graduation, Washington returned to Hampton to deliver a speech. During this speech, he expounded on the ideas that he would develop over the next quarter century. As he took the podium, speaking to his former professors, Washington described his faith and his vision of the South. He told the audience that racial progress would demand "not education merely, but also wisdom and common sense, a heart set on the right and a trust in God."[24] It was a simple message, but one rooted in compromise and collaboration.

Washington's speech at Hampton demonstrated that he was on the way to becoming a leader in the post-Reconstruction South. In this new South, no one might be canceled. Indeed, his speech at Hampton perfectly describes why he was the right man to lead Tuskegee: he worked hard to establish relationships with people who were often not fully committed to civil rights.

Tuskegee's emergence as a major African American town goes back to a deal between a former slave who was willing to deal with a political party that was not particularly friendly to Black people.

Lewis Adams was one of the important Black leaders of early Tuskegee. Born a slave around 1843, by 1880 the skilled shoemaker had established himself as a farmer and political boss of Tuskegee's Black community. During that year, two Democratic Party candidates for office asked him to support their candidacy. Adams endorsed them on the condition that they support a normal school for African Americans in Macon County. After their election, both politicians kept their promise and helped push a bill through the Alabama State House initiating what later became the Tuskegee Institute.

With the school authorized, Adams reached out to George Washington Campbell, an insurance broker and former slave master, to help him lay the groundwork for the institution. Campbell and Adams contacted Samuel Chapman Armstrong, founder of Hampton, to ask for suggestions for a leader of the new school. Chapman, remembering his former student, nominated Booker T. Washington, who became the school's first principal.[25]

Booker T. Washington continued the work Campbell and Adams did to protect the interests of the African American community in Tuskegee. Although he was restricted in how much he could advocate on behalf of his race, Tuskegee Institute nevertheless prospered. This resulted from a combination of self-determination and the cultivation of relationships Washington established with white men and women who either were interested in or could be persuaded to assist Black people. In order to fulfil his mission, Washington looked beyond others' faults. He wrote, "The Negro boys and girls of to-day need the help, the direction, and the personal sympathy and interest of the white people just as much as they ever did, if not more."[26]

At the same time Washington—while holding a public persona that appealed to segregationists—was secretly pushing for integration through the courts and often raised money for that cause.

Washington's belief in forgiveness was rooted in his faith. He believed that Black people should forgive white people and move toward reconciliation. When he was an old man seeing death in the not-too-distant future, Washington recalled his own experiences that had given him hope for change in his earlier years. He compared racism to his once-held religious denominational prejudice. At one time, he believed Baptists were the only true Christians. Education, meetings, and interactions with people from different church backgrounds persuaded him to move beyond that prejudice.

> "Till I was eleven years old, I believed with all my heart that nobody but a Baptist ever got to heaven. That idea wasn't argued out of me, but it got out gradually as I came in contact with good Methodists and other good people. I was the creature of circumstances."[27]

"TILL I WAS ELEVEN YEARS OLD, I BELIEVED WITH ALL MY HEART THAT NOBODY BUT A BAPTIST EVER GOT TO HEAVEN. THAT IDEA WASN'T ARGUED OUT OF ME, BUT IT GOT OUT GRADUALLY AS I CAME IN CONTACT WITH GOOD METHODISTS AND OTHER GOOD PEOPLE. I WAS THE CREATURE OF CIRCUMSTANCES."
—BOOKER T. WASHINGTON

Washington believed that if he could overcome his prejudice, white people could overcome their own racism through education and through interaction with Black people.

A City on a Hill

Throughout his life, Washington worked diligently to establish "a town built on a hill [that] cannot be hidden," the metaphor Jesus spoke of in the Bible for illuminating the world with God's truth (Matthew 5:14). Washington wanted to establish a Christian learning institution, and while he established Tuskegee as nonsectarian, he also saw it as a Christian institution. For example, in a letter he wrote to Ms. Lord in 1887, he took pleasure in how the Christian environment at Tuskegee led many students to the Lord:

> I can not close this letter without mentioning the wonderful religious interest existing in our school. Within the last week 106 students have become Christians. There are only a very few left now and the interest still continues.[28]

The number of conversions and Washington's enthusiasm about them reveals that this was Washington's plan all along. Seeing young people come to the Lord was the same plan that Washington had earlier prayed for while a student at Hampton. No wonder he took pleasure in seeing his hopes come to fruition at Tuskegee.

As a renowned leader in the Black community, Washington traveled the nation. He often spoke to missionary associations and encouraged them to reach out to everyone, particularly the poor. In 1887, he spoke at the Christian Endeavor Society and encouraged them to continue their missions to the African American community, reminding them that God does not respect or play favorites among people. Just as he did many times during his life, he recalled his early years in West Virginia and remembered how God had given him favor while he was a poor kid laboring in the region's coal and salt mines. As someone who rose from those humble beginnings because he found people willing to help and mentor him, he now demanded that Christians help the less fortunate regardless of their color or status. He stated:

> No person was to[o] Black or forsaken to make Christ ashamed to take him by the hand. All over this country there are promising boys and girls with Black skins who sink into the mire simply because no one has the Christian courage to take them by the hand and lift them up.[29]

Even though Washington did not speak often about civic equality, he was blunt about the fact that segregation and prejudice are sins.

> How often as a poor Black boy have I passed by the doors of churches and Sunday schools and heard the grand old song, 'Come to Jesus,' welling up from hundreds of throats, and at the same time if I, a poor Black boy, had obeyed the command, and entered that church or Sunday

school, I should have been put out by force, if necessary.[30]

Washington believed that the Black experience in America meant that the Bible had a special message for them. "The teaching of the Bible is just as necessary to the Negro in freedom as it was in slavery."[31] This is the theme he brought to Tuskegee. His dream was to create a space that prepared young men and women like Sunday school had done for him. To prepare citizens and, more importantly, prepare Christians to go out in the world, and to do good.

Even though he was busy running the institution and orating on the speaking circuit, he continued to set the model by reading the Bible and praying every day.[32]

Washington was confident that the legacy of the African American ancestors was the "great heritage that the fathers and others gained for him by blood and toil."[33] The legacy he spoke of was their faith. To affirm his ancestors required taking up the cross that they so faithfully carried. If the ancestors could preserve unshakable faith in slavery, Washington wanted to see that foundation continue to be preserved.

EVEN THOUGH HE WAS BUSY RUNNING THE INSTITUTION AND ORATING ON THE SPEAKING CIRCUIT, HE CONTINUED TO SET THE MODEL BY READING THE BIBLE AND PRAYING EVERY DAY.

Washington also saw it as the responsibility to the Black community to spread the gospel. Even though prison ministries are popular today, they were not as popular as places of ministry during Washington's time. Washington actively promoted prison ministries, stating:

> The people in the jails or in prison have had no chance; they are the ignorant, the ones who are away down, and it is our duty to take them by the hand through the church and Sunday-school and help to lift them up.[34]

To Booker T. Washington, Jesus provided the perfect model of leadership. Though born a slave, Washington never felt that being a servant was a problem. Washington found comfort in the reality that Jesus came to be a servant of humanity, and that whoever wants to become great among others must be a servant (Matthew 20:26).

Booker T. Washington was an exemplary man who was guided by his faith to do wonderful things in life. He also believed that forgiveness was central to reconciliation, and he longed for unity between the races in his time and context. His faith and humility led him to identify with the less fortunate throughout his life. Even though Booker T. Washington emerged as the most important Black leader of the early twentieth century, he never forgot his experiences as a slave and poor miner. Because of his faith, Washington left a legacy that remains intact today.

> **WASHINGTON FOUND COMFORT IN THE REALITY THAT JESUS CAME TO BE A SERVANT OF HUMANITY, AND THAT WHOEVER WANTS TO BECOME GREAT AMONG OTHERS MUST BE A SERVANT. (MATTHEW 20:26)**

Explore Your Faith with Harriet Tubman and Booker T. Washington

* James 1:22 tells us to not only listen to the Word of God but to do what it says. In what ways did Harriet Tubman listen and do this? What lessons about listening and doing do we learn from her journey?

* What does Tubman's life tell us about the power of prayer? The power of forgiveness?

* What does Booker T. Washington's life tell us about the importance of dialogue?

CHAPTER 4

FINDING OUR VOICE

You will seek me and find me when you seek me with all your heart.

JEREMIAH 29:13

Activist, writer, and intellectual W. E. B. Du Bois wrote:

> He and I came from different backgrounds. I
> was born free. Washington was born slave. He
> felt the lash of an overseer across his back. I was
> born in Massachusetts, he on a slave plantation
> in the South. My great-grandfather fought
> with the Colonial Army in New England in the
> American Revolution. [This earned the grand-
> father his freedom.] I had a happy childhood
> and acceptance in the community. Washing-
> ton's childhood was hard. I had many more
> advantages: Fisk University, Harvard, gradu-
> ate years in Europe. Washington had little for-
> mal schooling.[1]

In his last interview before his death, W. E. B. Du Bois had
finally realized that the great scholarly debate the two men
engaged in largely reflected their different backgrounds. As
we saw in the last chapter, Washington advocated for the Black
community by appealing to white moderates, not pushing too
hard for political and social rights. The more accommodation-
ist position Washington took was a reality of the times in which
Washington—as a Black man in the Deep South—lived.

Du Bois, who had once supported Washington, disagreed
with this position. In his seminal work, *The Souls of Black Folk*,
he devoted an entire chapter cataloguing his disagreement with
Washington. But Du Bois had never been a slave, and he came
from a prominent and free African American family. He was
educated in the best integrated schools, while Washington's

education began in impoverished Sunday schools and ended at Hampton. As he wrote that chapter, Du Bois accused Washington of giving up too much in terms of political and social equality. It is ironic that Du Bois made this accusation, understanding that Washington had once been owned.

The two men remained at odds for the remainder of their lives, just as much as they were separated by their births. Although Du Bois could not fully move beyond his differences with Washington, as he aged, he seemed to understand Washington much more. He recognized that Washington's voice was influenced by his experiences as a child just as the circumstances of Du Bois's early years had influenced him.

And yet, regardless of what Du Bois or Washington may have believed, the fact is that both men changed over the last stages of their lives. Indeed, God did not create any of us to be static beings. As we grow, we can mature and develop our own voices. For example, Washington in his last years pushed much harder for civil rights. He also spoke more forcefully about his Christian faith. After 1915, Du Bois became more open to black nationalism, aligning more with Washington's views. Ironically, he even came close to Washington's stance on the need for Black people to turn inward to develop and maintain their own culture and communities.

Washington's and Du Bois' lives are examples of the importance of reflection and finding our voice. Even though we are influenced by circumstances of class and upbringing, as we develop our own voice, we often change. Communities can also find their voices as they reexamine attitudes and prejudices. In the early twentieth century, many transitions led Black people to reexamine their voice not only for themselves but also for their communities as a whole.

Our faith is part of our voice as well. It can sometimes be difficult to express that aspect of our voice. This may be due to the society we live in, or it may be our own insecurity with our faith. We may fear being classified as intolerant or on the wrong side of history. When we have such fears, it is often the result of static faith. Perhaps we are struggling to find our Christian voice in a world where such voices are not welcomed, and we are reluctant to speak. Maybe we have the voice but have not learned to trust it yet.

Migrations

Booker T. Washington's death in 1915 came at an important period in African American history. The rest of the world was engulfed in a war that the United States would not enter until 1917. The year that Washington died, film director and producer D. W. Griffith released *Birth of a Nation*. Adapted from Thomas Dixon's novel, *The Clansman*, the movie was Hollywood's first major blockbuster. As the title of the book confirms, the film is a racist account of the rise of the Ku Klux Klan during the Reconstruction period. The film was even screened in the White House. President Woodrow Wilson thought that the film was fantastic and apparently gave the film his stamp of approval.[2] The popularity of the film had deadly consequences. It led to the revival of the Ku Klux Klan, which gained tremendous popularity in the years after *Birth of a Nation*.

The Klan's revival happened at a time when the lynching of African Americans remained commonplace. In 1916, one of the most terrifying examples of a lynching occurred in Waco, Texas. On May 15 of that year, more than ten thousand men, women, and children watched approvingly as Jesse Washington was tortured and lynched. After the mob lynched Washington, they burned him while the rest of those gathered watched and cheered.

I can only imagine how African Americans felt in this period. I think about African American soldiers, who had served their nation with distinction, faced such severe racism and discrimination. One such disturbing case happened in Houston, Texas. When a Black soldier tried to protect a Black woman from being assaulted by a white police officer, it lead to the arrest of many soldiers and caused a race riot. In the aftermath, more than one hundred Black soldiers were arrested and tried. Nineteen Black soldiers were hung.

Despite this terror, Black people continued to make strides forward. African Americans and a few progressive white Americans created a number of organizations to attempt to turn the tide. Notable among these societies were the National Association for the Advancement of Colored People (NAACP) formed in 1909, and the National Urban League established in 1910.

Even though African Americans faced increasing scrutiny of their political and social privileges during the first few decades of the twentieth century, this period also witnessed a flowering of Black culture. In cities such as Washington, DC, Boston, Harlem, and Chicago, the emergence of a Black cultural and social movement was particularly strong. In Boston, for example, Josephine St. Pierre Ruffin founded the *Women's Era* in 1894— the first African American newspaper in America specifically for Black women. Ruffin, a middle-class woman, used the newspaper to pursue women's rights and respectability.

The newspaper promoted the importance of Black women organizing together into various women's clubs and organizations. The club movement was a major movement among Black women during the late nineteenth and early twentieth century. The largest club was the National Association of Colored Women (NACW) formed in 1896. As an organization, the NACW fought for equal rights and led the struggle for an anti-lynching law. At the same time, the organization was an opportunity for middle- and upper-class Black women to come together.

Ida B. Wells was the most prominent woman involved in the club movement. Like most leaders of the club movement, religious faith was the foundation of her activism. Raised as a Methodist, she was a member of Mother Bethel AME Church in Chicago, when Reverend Reverdy C. Ransom was the pastor. Ransom was a strong supporter of civil rights and opposed most of Booker T. Washington's agenda. Ransom wanted immediate civil equality. This disagreement with Washington led Ransom to work with W. E. B. Du Bois and William Monroe Trotter to help found the Niagara Movement in 1905.[3] The Niagara Movement was a group of African American men who wanted to push for immediate civil rights.

Wells left the AME Church after a scandal involving some of the church leaders. The scandal did not involve Wells. Even after leaving her denomination, she quickly found another church and started serving there. Of her commitment to the church she writes, "I had been brought up in a Christian home under the influence of the Sunday school and church and I wanted to bring my children up in the same way."[4] In her new church, Wells taught Sunday school. There she and a few students from her Sunday school class formed the Negro Fellowship League. This organization linked Christian principles with social action. First and foremost, the organization wanted to help poorer African Americans in Chicago. The league found other supporters in some of the other women's clubs in Chicago, such as the Gaudeamus Charity Club whose membership included Grace Wilson, the first Black woman to hold a civil service position in the city.[5]

Ida Wells was active in numerous other organizations and also helped to found the Tourgee Club (later named the Ida B. Wells club). The members of the Tourgee Club wanted to improve the lives of Black residents of Chicago and promote the kingdom of God. The Tourgee Club was influential in the creation of an African American orchestra in Chicago and in the operation of a kindergarten serving African American children at Mother Bethel.

Black women also formed sororities and other clubs throughout America, from Alpha Kappa Alpha to Delta Sigma Theta, and also took a role in promoting the arts. Myra Hemmings organized the Phillis Wheatley Dramatic Guild Players in San Antonio during the 1920s. As a result of this artistic community, Spencer Williams, the preeminent Black film director of the 1940s, produced and filmed several movies on the city's eastside with Black actors from the city.

As a result of the hard work done by African Americans, between 1870 and 1900 African Americans closed the racial gap in land ownership and homeownership substantially. However, after 1915, Black land ownership peaked in the South.

Increasingly, groups such as the white caps terrorized African Americans and forced many off their land. Particularly pervasive in Mississippi, persons involved in white capping were white farmers, often from the poorer agricultural and tenant farming class, who felt compromised by Southern industrialization. While the white cap societies in the South were unaffiliated with the Ku Klux Klan, like the Klan their members held racist beliefs. The white caps, believed that merchants, Black farmers, and tenants were conspiring to destroy their economic opportunities and push them into sharecropping and tenant farming. They led campaigns to push African Americans from the land they lived on and often resorted to violence to achieve their goals.

The violence forced many Black people out of the rural South. Tens of thousands of them moved to cities such as Atlanta and Tulsa. The migration to urban cities over the first decades of the twentieth century was the beginning of a period when Black people became a much more urban community. Most of the migrants, however, found their way out of the South entirely.

The migration out of the South that occurred in the years following World War I changed the trajectory of Black landholding. With hundreds of thousands of Blacks leaving the rural South for urban locations in the North and West as part of the Great Migration, Black-owned farms became a distant memory for many.[6]

Finding a Voice

The first part of the Great Migration occurred between 1916 and 1940 as 1.6 million African Americans moved out of the

South, mostly to northern cities. While most expected a *Canaan Promised Land* of sorts, what they experienced were jobs that provided little pay, and racial and class discrimination they were forced to endure.

Leaving home requires one to start over. It's hard, whether you're heading to college, or accepting a position that requires you to relocate. When I had to leave my parents in order to move to Atlanta for graduate school, and when my wife, Almie, left home in the Philippines for America, we did not know the obstacles we would experience.

Leaving home exerts a psychological toll. It means leaving friends and family, who also experience loss, and may feel left behind. Through their churches and other organizations, African American Christians led the way in trying to help new emigrants during the Great Migration. Middle-class African Americans worried about the impoverished conditions of the new migrants.

Club women worried that without mentorship the recent migrants would end up "poor, destitute, and desperate in society with no place to work or live."[7] In 1922, the Phillis Wheatley Club, the organization of upper-middle-class Black women, decided to do something to help people who, according to the club, were being led "unaware into disreputable homes, entertainment and employment because of lack of the protection that strange girls of other races enjoy." The club worked with local churches to help provide a place of sanctuary for young Black women and their families.

In order to help the newcomers in the city, the club set up a nursery at the Trinity AME Church. In addition to helping poorer mothers and their children, the club also wanted to clean up the entire neighborhood. Believing that local saloons in the Black community, particularly those near Black schools, were not good for young people, the club led campaigns aimed to shut down local saloons.[8]

If You See My Savior

Thomas A. Dorsey, Duke Ellington, and Ethel Waters were three individuals who understood the difficulty of these times. In leaving home, they experienced success but found their new opportunities ultimately unfulfilling. They struggled initially to find their identity. In the end, they learned that they needed to strengthen their relationship with God in order to ground their lives. When they finally did, they also found their voice, and the peace they had looked for all along their journey.

Thomas A. Dorsey was one of the 1.6 million African Americans to move to urban cities during the Great Migration. A native of rural Georgia, Dorsey was raised in a very religious home. His father was a Christian minister, and his mother was also deeply religious and a musician. When he was young, Dorsey's family was part of a group that left the rural South for urban locations. Dorsey's father was a college-educated man unable to turn his education into a middle-class existence.

The reality that college did not translate to a meaningful financial future likely had an impact on young Thomas, who dropped out of school at thirteen to pursue a career in music. The young man took a different career path than his father; instead of the ministry, he perfected his craft in blues and ragtime music while surrounded by drugs and prostitution in the bordellos and saloons of Atlanta's African American red-light district.[9]

In 1916, Dorsey left Atlanta to find work in Philadelphia's naval yards. Even though America had not yet entered World War I, the war effort created economic opportunities for Black people. African American newspapers such as the *Chicago Defender* encouraged African Americans in the South to leave their homes and seek the better jobs in the North. When America entered the war in 1917, the number of jobs available to African Americans increased even more, leading to more migration to northern cities.

On his way to Philadelphia, Dorsey decided to visit his family in Chicago. There he experienced Bronzeville, the location of the largest African American community in Chicago, and recognized that the South Side of Chicago provided myriad opportunities for blues musicians like himself. Dorsey quickly became a regular musician playing at rent parties and buffet flats. Rent parties were gatherings where tenants hired musicians to play at their apartment. The tenants also invited guests to come listen to the music for a fee. The money raised would be used to pay the apartment's rent. Buffet flats were illegal speakeasies and brothels located in apartments or homes that were partitioned into different flats.

Dorsey made good money, but the lifestyles of many of the people he encountered at these gatherings made him uncomfortable. He had joined the Pilgrim Baptist Church in Chicago soon after he arrived in the city. Dorsey also took classes at the Chicago School of Composition and Arranging. Both of those involvements demonstrate that he wanted to be more than a blues and jazz player and wanted to make a living at more "moral" establishments.[10]

Dorsey wanted to move away from the seedy establishments when he accepted a position as choir director at New Hope Baptist Church in Morgan Park, a location where many of the older and more established Black Chicagoans lived. While it appeared that Dorsey was on the straight and narrow, there was one problem. Money. The church did not pay him well. Actually, the church did not even pay him regularly. For Dorsey, someone who had pursued the blues life and rejected the religious life of his father, who could never make enough money to provide a decent lifestyle for his family, the lack of money was a problem. Dorsey needed money to survive, and at this time, the best way for him to make it was still in the blues scene. Therefore, he left his choir director position and went back to the bordellos and rent parties where he was paid regularly.

The conflict in his spirit was still strong. Even though he had played the blues his entire adult life, the influence of his Christian parents and his own faith remained. He started writing spiritual songs. And in 1924, he published his second Christian song, "We Will Meet Him in the Sweet By and By." This song had some success and even appeared in the *Baptist Hymnal* for that year.[11]

Even though he had success writing and arranging religious music, he could not earn the money he needed to survive. Furthermore, the temptations connected with the blues were strong. Ma Rainey, one of the most popular blues musicians of all time, heard of Dorsey's talent and hired him to accompany her on tour. The opportunity was too good to turn down. Life on tour was basically the *sporting life*, referring to a life that revolves around often illegal establishments of gambling, sports events, and red-light districts.

The pressures of living the sporting life versus the life that God wanted Dorsey to live led him to a crisis. His recent marriage and birth of a child must have made his decision to tour with Rainey even harder. But the money he made allowed him to support his family. It was hard enough for Dorsey to leave his family on Friday and Saturday nights to play in the red-light districts of Chicago. But on Sunday morning he went to church with his family.

To go on tour with Ma Rainey was a blues musician's dream. But it also came with conflict. The smell of the marijuana smoke, the temptations of gambling, and the permissive sexual practices of the men and women who visited the buffet flats where Rainey and her band hung out were a moral challenge for the married family man.

It did not take long for the contradictions of his life to lead Thomas to a breakdown. In 1926, the pressures of his double life finally became too much, and he suffered a mental breakdown that required his hospitalization. Sitting in the hospital, Dorsey reached out to God once more. Struggling to feel normal again, he prayed to God for forgiveness and another opportunity to make it right. Eventually, he felt well enough to be released from the hospital, and he tried to get away from the lure of money and the blues. He went back to the church and was prayed over by the elders.

Dorsey knew that God wanted him to commit to playing gospel music. When he realized that he could use the same blues progressions in gospel music, Dorsey recovered from his mental

UNSHAKABLE FAITH

collapse. He began incorporating the blues into new music, laying the groundwork for the genre of modern gospel. His first song, "If You See My Savior," is basically a blues song underpinned by Christian lyrics.

The blues often explores the emotions of longing and pain. "If You See My Savior" tells the story of a man visiting a sick friend. The narrator asks the dying friend to speak to Jesus on his behalf; he is struggling with something and longs for someone to intercede for him. Considering Dorsey's mental state at the time he wrote the song, it was a perfect metaphor for someone like him who was also seeking the Lord's intercession.[12]

At the Cross

"If You See My Savior" did not sell well. Chicago's churches were reluctant to play the song not simply because it sounded like a blues song, but also because of Dorsey's blues background. This was part of Dorsey's experiences with "church folk" and how "sinners" are pushed out of the church. This dynamic is as relevant today as it was during Dorsey's time.

One can only think about what would have happened if the early Christians had successfully pushed out Paul because of his past persecution of them, rather than embrace the converted apostle. Too many times, people come to the church needing help but, instead of receiving that encouragement, they find the doors shut in their faces. People are pushed away because of their politics, ethnicity, or other manner that discomforts some. Such was the case for Dorsey. After experiencing depression, he desperately needed the love and support of the church community. But the community he needed was not ready to accept him.

While feeling abandoned, he leaned back into the blues life.

In the gospel accounts of the temptation of Jesus, Satan tempted Jesus twice before he took Him to a high mountain and offered Him everything if He would worship him (Matthew 4; Luke 4). The message is clear: the Enemy knows our weaknesses and is always trying to exploit them. For Dorsey, it was not the blues *music* that was problematic. It was the *lifestyle* and the temptations that came with it. What made the temptations worse were the profits that came from that lifestyle.

Falling into temptation, Dorsey made one final foray into that life. He had developed a friendship with guitarist Hudson Whittaker, another accompanist for Ma Rainey. The two men started writing and arranging songs together. One night, Whittaker came up with the lyrics for a song filled with references to sex and promiscuity. Dorsey liked the lyrics and quickly sat down at the piano to come up with the music to go along with them. When he completed the song, Dorsey on piano and Whittaker on the slide guitar practiced the song and quickly knew they had a hit. The song was catchy, and the music track sounded great. They rushed to a music studio to record and copyright the song.

When the song was released, it was a massive hit. After years of struggle, Dorsey, now using the alias *Georgia Tom* in blues circles, was a major star. People knew and sang the lyrics all across the nation. And with that he was making the kind of money he had always wanted. If he kept up this lifestyle, he would be set for life.[13]

He went on tour with Whittaker—but the Lord continued to pursue Thomas. Dorsey made stops at churches to promote his gospel songs while on tour. He knew God was waiting, but the money seemed too good for him to surrender, until 1932 when Dorsey decided he did not want to continue performing in the blues world and would make another attempt to fully devote his life to writing and recording Christian music. Since 1930, he had made some inroads with local churches and congregations, and the churches in Chicago gradually opened up to his Christian music.

Change was coming, particularly in churches in urban America. In Chicago, the Great Migration contributed to the increase in city residents from the Holiness and Pentecostal traditions. A Pentecostal denomination, the Church of God in Christ (COGIC), in particular, experienced tremendous growth during the years after 1914. The formation of Chicago's COGIC churches started that year when a group of Black women requested COGIC Bishop Charles Harrison Mason to send a pastor to Chicago.

The new migrants brought their "country" traditions to the city where they often felt out of place in the more established Baptist, Presbyterian, and Episcopal churches. The more established churches often shunned the playing of drums and sanctified singing, speaking in tongues, and bodily expressions in church. In contrast, the Holiness and Pentecostal churches embraced these forms of worship. Therefore, in Chicago's storefront churches and in prayer groups, African Americans from working-class backgrounds were developing their voices in a way that mirrored the improvisational beginnings of jazz and blues music.

Through extemporaneous prayers and religious experiences, Black people's voices expressed their fears, hopes, and their faith in the most honest way. They developed a religious tradition that reflected the church and Black community roots in the Negro spiritual. In storefront churches and prayer groups all across urban America, Black people were expressing everything they felt in their heart. The pain, the sorrow—and the joy in the Lord—all found their way into this prayer and worship style filled with groans, moans, and shouts.

Recording Voices

While the Holiness and Pentecostal churches spread in urban cities, the 1920s brought other changes to the musical landscape. In 1920, Mamie Smith went into an OKeh music studio in New York City and recorded several blues songs. Smith's recordings generated tremendous interest in the African American communities, leading OKeh Records to draft other Black talent. Other record companies followed suit and led an explosion in what we now refer to as *race records*, produced for the African American community. While blues and jazz records predominated the recordings in the first six years after Smith's recording, some companies sought out religious songs and Christian ministers to record.

These early recordings did not reflect the improvisational and emotional content of the blues and jazz recordings. This would change in 1926 when OKeh Records commissioned Arizona Dranes, a blind woman from Texas, who had already gained a following in COGIC circles, to travel to Chicago and record a series of tracks.

On June 16, 1926, Dranes sat down at a piano and struck its black and white keys with a spiritual passion few people outside the Pentecostal and Holiness churches had heard before. In that first session, she recorded six songs. These *sanctified* songs are generally considered the first true modern gospel songs ever recorded. The short recordings lasted roughly three minutes. Spirit-filled, Dranes, with her friends surrounding her at the piano, was not thinking about the recording; she was playing the way she did in church. With her grunts, staccato piano playing, and foot stomps, Dranes created a recording about as close to sanctified as there had ever been. What Mamie Smith did for blues music by opening the doors for a generation of performers, Dranes did for sanctified, Holy Ghost–inspired music.[14]

Dranes's recordings sold well in the Black community, a fact that led other record companies to seek out other sanctified music acts. She also collaborated with ministers and musicians. In what was perhaps her last recording in 1929, Dranes collaborated on a recording of a sermon in Dallas, Texas, with Pentecostal preacher Reverend Joe Lenley. Dranes would not record another song after 1929, but remained a mainstay on the Pentecostal music scene until the 1940s. After that, little more is known about her until her death in 1963. Dranes's influence could be found in the new generation of singers that followed, including in the gospel music of Clara Ward and Mahalia Jackson.

Local radio stations began playing recordings not only of Black gospel but also of Black Church services. By the early 1930s, All Nations Pentecostal, led by Elder Lucy Smith, had their services broadcast in Chicago. These broadcasts took sanctified music and preaching to the African American mainstream.[15]

The changes in musical interests that were fortified with the advent of gospel recordings gave Dorsey another opportunity to pursue his dream to be a gospel music composer and performer. But it would take another traumatic experience in his life to finally push Dorsey to fully surrender his life to Christ. In 1932, his wife and son died. Probably fearing another breakdown, Dorsey sought solace in his music. At this spiritual crossroads, he thought about his loss, sat down at his piano, and started to improvise. The melody arose for "Must Jesus Bear the Cross Alone."

This sacred hymn details the trials all Christians have, expressing the reality that we carry burdens. While Dorsey played the melody and pondered its meaning, he transitioned to something completely new with a different melody. The words "precious Lord, take my hand" came to his mind. Dorsey and his associate wrote the lyrics to the song, which in time would become the most recognized gospel song ever. For Dorsey, this marked an end to his involvement in the blues world and his formal, full-time introduction into the emerging field of Black gospel music. Dorsey became the standard-bearer of this new musical genre.[16]

As Dorsey's life illustrates, although we may fall many times, God is constantly giving us opportunities for renewal. In truth, we can relapse in our sin. For some people, it's drugs. For others, it's sexual sin and infidelity. For others, it may be lying or something else. For Thomas Dorsey, it was money and his reliance on it for sustenance. Apparently, church people were reluctant to mentor him in his time of need and this should challenge us as Christians.

We are to examine ourselves regularly to ensure that our doors and hearts are open to those who need us. We can ask ourselves if we are available and praying for the relapsed drug addict. Are we there for the cheater? What about the dealer or hustler? Are we there for the abused? What about the racist? Can we open our hearts to them? Sometimes the sinner that needs to be forgiven is us. Do we have love in our hearts to forgive ourselves? God calls us to be loving, and that includes the person we see when we look in the mirror.

His Eye Is on the Sparrow

Ethel Waters is one of the most important African American vocalists and performers of all time, though she is much less known compared to her contemporaries, such as Bessie Smith, Ma Rainey, and Billie Holiday. Had Waters died early in life, she might be seen as part of that group of legends. In many ways, Waters's life still mirrors the tragic life of Billie Holiday. Billie Holiday was raped as a young child and turned to prostitution by the time she was fourteen. She became a heroin addict and was dead at forty-four years old.

Waters's musical legacy: she was a bridge between blues singers like Ma Rainey and Bessie Smith, and more jazz-influenced singers such as Billie Holiday and Ella Fitzgerald. In her early years, Waters sang with Bessie Smith, who was already an established blues singer. Waters developed a different style from Smith and other blues singers. Her voice was not as powerful as Smith's and Rainey's. And she did not have the improvisational timing of Billie Holiday. What Waters did have was a remarkably clear tone and the ability to sing pop tunes.

Ethel Waters recorded numerous popular hits including "Am I Blue," "Dinah," and "Saint Louis Blues." She also recorded with the most important artists of the period, including Duke Ellington. In 1932, both performers were at the peak of their popularity when they recorded "I Can't Give You Anything But Love." The next year, Waters recorded "Stormy Weather," the song that established her as a pop superstar.

Waters—who, along with her ongoing recording successes, had a standout career in theater—transitioned to film in the 1930s. Even though we may see her roles as stereotypical today, they were quite progressive at the time. Her roles did not fit into the traditional mammy, jezebel, or tragic mulatto tropes that Black women were all too often forced into. Film historian Donald Bogle writes that Waters "was one of the first Black stars to take her music into the cultural mainstream and to infuse American popular culture with her jazzy/bluesy pop diva style."[17] As time passed, she successfully transitioned on screen from roles for younger woman to a more maternal role and eschewed the traditional mammy part.

In 1943, she was selected to play Petunia in the screen version of *Cabin in the Sky* (she was also this character in the theater production). The movie was a major success, opening up opportunities for African Americans in film in the same way that she had opened doors in theater and in music a generation earlier.

Stormy Weather

Ethel Waters's professional success masked a very troubled life. In her autobiography, *His Eye Is on the Sparrow*, first published in 1951, Waters describes her difficult childhood. At the time of its publication, she was over fifty years of age, and continued to enjoy tremendous success. In that year of publication, Waters became the first Black woman to play a lead role in a television show when she played the title role in *Beulah*. The year before, she received excellent reviews for her performance in *Pinky*, even receiving an Academy Award nomination for Best Supporting Actress.

Waters was born in 1900 in Chester, Pennsylvania. Her parents were not married. They were not even in a relationship. In her autobiography, Waters informs us that she was the child of rape. Her mother and her family lived in the poorer section of town. According to Waters, at the time of her birth they lived in an alley where youth was often stolen from young girls and boys. "My aunts, my mother, and Charlie had to bring themselves up. . . . They lived in an alley, and the boys were around the house all the time. When my grandmother was home on her day off they'd watch for her to leave and then would return."[18]

According to Water's description of life in Chester, sexual abuse was widespread and a major threat for young girls. Although her mother, Louise, was a woman of deep religious faith, the traps of the community took their toll. Waters's father was from a middle-class family who lived on the better side of town. He was also a sexual predator. Waters's aunt knew his intentions, but the family did nothing to protect her sister Louise from being raped. Upon learning of her daughter's pregnancy, her mother punished her. Waters's paternal family denied any rape had occurred, although they did acknowledge the child. Not surprisingly, Ethel's mother "resented my father and never afterward would have anything to do with him."[19]

Ethel had limited interaction with her paternal family. The pain of the situation was too great for the family to handle. Even

when she met her grandmother years later, the situation was difficult. Ethel wrote, "I was taken to Lydia Waters' big home uptown.
She seemed sad on seeing me, but I wasn't much moved. The
resemblance I bore her was unmistakable, but my chief feeling
was one of not wishing her to touch me." Even then, Waters spoke
of her faith. She wrote, "I felt that God would always be with me,
helping as I battled my way through that wasteland of violent
emotions and exploding egos in which I was growing up."[20]

Waters believed that one of the reasons that her relationship
with her mother was so strained was the striking similarity of
her features to her father's. This had to have been traumatic for
both of them, especially since her own mother was unable to
demonstrate any sense of emotion or concern for her throughout her entire life—with the exception being during her last
days. Since Ethel's mother was unable to care for her, therefore,
the raising of Ethel was basically relegated to her grandmother.
Her grandmother was a very religious woman, who did not
have a husband or anyone to help her raise little Ethel. Indeed,
the family was but one of the many families of unskilled Black
laborers struggling to survive in early twentieth–century Chester, Pennsylvania.[21]

Good paying jobs were largely unavailable to Black women.
Ethel's family, headed by women, was poor. Rarely during her
years growing up did Ethel spend more than a few weeks in one
place. Instead, her childhood was spent in a series of tenements
and row houses. Waters stated that "in crowded slum homes
one's sex education begins very early indeed. Mine began when
I was about three and sleeping in the same room, often in the
same bed, with my aunts and my transient uncles."[22]

Waters's family lived in red-light districts, and her home life was so difficult that she often slept in the streets because the streets were "no more uncomfortable than the broken-down beds, with treacherous springs or the bedbug-infested pallets we had at home."[23] It would have been easy for Waters to turn to drugs and prostitution. In her early years, she lived as almost a street kid. Thankfully, Waters never turned to drugs and prostitution, though she did succumb to other temptations of the streets. She admitted that she became a petty thief, was a lookout for prostitutes, also ran errands for the local prostitutes, and knew and interacted with local pimps regularly.

Not all of her family members escaped prostitution and drugs. One family member, Blanche, is in Waters's autobiography, and was Ethel's close friend and playmate. Blanche was in and out of Ethel's life until Blanche was roughly twelve years old, when she turned to prostitution and later drugs. Sadly, by Blanche's teenage years, she had contracted syphilis. "In the last stages of her life, and still not twenty years old, she took to sniffing coke and using the bang needles to forget the pain."[24] The realities of drug use were something that Waters saw repeatedly during her childhood.

However, soon after she left their home on Clifton Street, she was able to go to a Catholic school. Her grandmother was Catholic and wanted to instill religious values in her granddaughter. Her mother, Louise, who came in and out of her life regularly, did not want her to go to a Catholic school because she was Protestant.[25]

Even though she lived in a rough environment where prostitution, drug addiction, and crime were common, Waters found her solace in the Lord. At eleven years old, she became much more interested in the church and in exploring her relationship with God. She believed that God could transform people and cleanse their sins. She just wasn't sure that this grace was available for her. She would later write that it was at this age, during a children's revival, that she "truly came to know and to reverence Christ the redeemer."[26] As her relationship with the Lord developed, she understood that she wanted to be forgiven for her sins. She approached the mourner's bench at a church revival—at evangelical churches, a seat where people come to pray to receive Christ or to confess their sins. She wrote, "And then it happened! The peace of heart and of mind, the peace I had been seeking all my life." For the child who did not feel loved at home, she found in Christ "an ally, a friend close by to strengthen me and cheer me on."[27]

Yet something would cause Ethel to lose the enthusiasm of her early conversion. We know that many people, who embrace their newfound faith with much enthusiasm, can drift away a short time later. Sometimes there is a disconnect with people in the church. In Ethel Waters's case, it was an argument with another youth that challenged her devotion and left her disillusioned. There had been an argument that led her back to feeling unworthy and wondering how God could love someone like her. Waters became disillusioned about the church.

Simply stated, Waters did not feel that she was good enough for God. Considering all of the issues Waters dealt with and all of the bad influences in her life, it's not surprising she fell into disillusionment and depression. As she moved into adulthood, her church attendance became irregular, although she wrote, "I talk a great deal to Jesus. Often, He is my only playmate."[28]

Although Waters was not a regular churchgoer during the first fifty years of life, she was a Christian believer who readily acknowledged that God got her through difficult times. Indeed, there were many of them—particularly during her abusive first marriage. It's not surprising that the woman born of rape and living amid those who were pimps and prostitutes ended up in an abusive relationship. She married at thirteen years of age to a man twice her age. The relationship was abusive. Waters regretted the marriage, and within a year, she had left him.[29]

Without much education or marketable skills, Waters became a performer on the vaudeville circuit. Throughout the performing circuit, she was surrounded by people living the sporting life. While much of the sporting life would have been seductive—and, surely, drew her in often—she relied on God to protect her:

> We [African Americans are close] to this earth and to God. Shut up in ghettos, sneered at, beaten, enslaved, we have always answered our oppressors with brave singing, dancing, and laughing. Our greatest eloquence, the pith of the joy and sorrow in our unbreakable hearts, comes when we lift up our faces and talk to God, person to person. Ours is the truest dignity of man, the dignity of the undefeated.[30]

Accepting God's Love

Ethel Waters was unable to fully accept God's love during her first fifty years of life, though God was always for her. Her professional success gave her the ability to buy the things that she never had during her youth. She provided her family with financial stability and a stable place to live. She also finally developed a relationship with her mother. At the same time, her professional and personal success did not compensate for her lack of self-worth.

Waters knew God, but she had never fully surrendered to Him as an adult. Every time she wanted to, she thought about who she was, the circumstances of her birth, and the things she had done. When she looked at her life, she hated herself. It often takes hitting rock bottom to humble us. It would take a series of crises in Waters's life to lead a much older and more mature Ethel back to the mourner's bench she had not approached since her teenage years. Not only would she find God's grace right there, but she found her true mission in life.

Waters reached her low point in 1957. Although in her younger years she was remarkably thin and even had the nickname "Sweet Mama Stringbean," her weight had reached 350 pounds. She found performing difficult and worried about becoming a stereotype, a particular one that she had fought her entire life. Waters wrote in her second autobiography that she feared she was to her audience "their big, fat, comforting Mama image, who could—even as old and fat as she was—still be counted on to make them laugh and cry and forget their troubles for a little while."[31]

No trope has had a longer shelf life in American history than the Black mammy character and caricature. It is a stereotype that Black women have fought hard to overcome. Once athletic and slender, Ethel Waters feared that she could only find work portraying the mammy. The situation led her to a crisis. She knew the Lord, but as a sixty-year-old woman, she had not completely submitted to him. Additionally, like many of us, she was unable to look beyond her past and her self-image, to accept herself.

She still saw herself as the illegitimate child of rape who "was a ring leader of street gangs and street life in the slums."[32] Even though the circumstances of her early life were not her fault, she hated herself. Waters believed that she "had let the Lord down." Stripped of everything she had relied on to sustain her, she reached out to God in her emptiness and need. At the time of her contemplation, she learned that evangelist Billy Graham was in town with his crusade. Waters decided to attend and recommitted herself to the Lord at the event. She also became a part of Graham's crusades, singing and giving her testimony for the next twenty years. Waters finally embraced that Jesus loves us all just as we are. When she experienced and embraced God's love through Jesus, Ethel truly became blessed, finally accepted herself, and found the peace and contentment she had been searching for her entire life.

When we feel depressed or regret the things we have done, we must remind ourselves that Jesus still loves us. The apostle John confirmed: "But if we walk in the light, as he is in the light, we have fellowship with one another, and the blood of Jesus, his Son, purifies us from all sin" (1 John 1:7).

Duke Ellington: In My Solitude

Many Americans know very little about the life or the depth of accomplishments of Duke Ellington, one of America's greatest

composers. He was a leading composer of jazz music responsible for some of the most well-known big-band jazz classics.
While he enjoyed life, Ellington was very protective of his pri-
vacy. On stage he often seemed quiet. A skilled pianist, Ellington had a talent for writing hooks and songs that linked to a
person's inner spirit. His musical repertoire included songs that
one could dance to like "It Don't Mean a Thing (If It Ain't Got
That Swing)." It also included songs such as "Sophisticated
Lady" that speaks to a woman's elegance. He also wrote songs
like "Creole Love Call," a song that bordered on the sensual.

When Duke Ellington and Ethel Waters collaborated on two
major hit songs in the early 1930s, "Stormy Weather" and "I
Can't Give You Anything But Love," it appeared that the two
were entirely different people in terms of their lifestyles. Compared to Waters, Ellington had an extremely privileged upbringing, as he was born to an upper-middle-class family that was part
of the Black elite in Washington, DC. James Edward Ellington,
his father, was a butler for a prominent doctor. His connections
extended to the White House, as he was a butler for President
Harding on several occasions. Duke Ellington remarked that
his father "always acted as though he had money, whether he had
it or not. He spent and lived like a man who had money, and he
raised his family as though he were a millionaire.[33]

Duke Ellington's mother, Daisy Kennedy Ellington, also
came from a middle-class background. According to Ellington,
his father always wanted to buy the nicest things for her. Duke
Ellington was closer to his mother, who had a more significant
impact on his life. It was his mother who introduced him to the
Lord. As Ellington reflected many years later, he recalled his

mother repeatedly telling him that he was "blessed."[34] Of her, he said:

> She was mainly interested in knowing and understanding about God, and she painted the most wonderful word pictures of God. Every Sunday, she took me to at least two churches, usually to the Nineteenth Street Baptist, the church of her family, and to John Wesley A.M.E. Zion, my father's family church. It was never made clear to me that they were of different denominations, and to her, I'm sure, it did not matter. They both preached God, Jesus Christ, and that was the most important thing.[35]

Ellington went to Sunday school, and he wrote that learning about the Word provided him with a sense of "security." *Believing* for Ellington meant *belonging* to a greater community, something special, something loving and forgiving. These foundations remained with Ellington throughout his life. As a child growing up in the DC metropolis, Duke Ellington had many influences. Living in the Shaw neighborhood, the Black community in the Northwest area of the city, Duke Ellington had opportunities unheard of for most young African Americans during that time.

Washington, DC, was a *tour de force* that represented the hopes and aspirations of the African American bourgeois class. In the years after the Civil War, prominent African Americans had moved there seeking better opportunities. The following Black political leaders lived in the Shaw neighborhood at times during their lives: Blanche Bruce, one of the first two Black senators in the nation; P. B. S. Pinchback, former Black governor of Louisiana; Frederick Douglass; and William Calvin Chase, the editor of the *Washington Bee*.

Washington, DC, was also home to some of the most prominent Black women: Mary Church Terrell, the first president of the National Association of Colored Women, whose headquarters was located in DC, also the first Black woman in the nation to be elected to a local school board; Josephine Bruce, a local socialite, was involved in a number of Black women's organizations.

Howard University, formed in the years after the Civil War, became the educational mecca of the region. DC was also home to many Black scholars, such as the educator, author, and first Black Rhodes Scholar Alain Locke and professor at Howard; and the mathematician, sociologist, and influential author Kelly Miller. It would be in this metropolis that Locke, looking around at the prominence of African Americans in DC during his time there, probably formed some of his ideas about the *New Negro* that would soon be printed in his article entitled "Harlem: Mecca of the New Negro." The *New Negro* is a term used in Locke's essay that defines a new outlook among African American in the 1920s. It referred to a person who was conscious of and had pride in his or her past and was looking forward to a bright future. For Locke, that meant contending the lies of the ideology (lost cause) of the happy and contented slave and African American and centering Black life on truth.[36]

Ellington attended high school at the Armstrong Manual Training School, one of the two Black high schools in DC. The other one was M Street High school, which later became Dunbar High School. At school and at home, Ellington was exposed to the arts. It was important to his mother that he be properly trained as a pianist and, in his case, that meant learning how to read music. To this effort, she paid for piano tutors for the young Duke. Although he was just as interested in sports, even before he reached his teens, music and art were important pieces of his life.[37]

The nightlife was another influence on Ellington. Even before he reached maturity, Ellington frequented burlesque shows and local juke joints. Such exposure to these types of places was not a wholesome endeavor, and it may have contributed to Ellington's later social problems. At the same time, the musicians at the burlesque shows were some of the best in town. There, Duke Ellington learned about music performance and the art of working an audience. He also perfected his chord progressions and improvisational skills.

Ellington also visited local pool halls, particularly Frank Holliday's. Right next to the Howard Theater that brought in the best African American acts in the country, the young and impressionable Ellington had the opportunity there to meet and be mentored by some of the most notable pianists of the period. Ellington experienced Fats Waller and James P. Johnson, who often played sets at the pool hall after performing at the Howard Theater.[38] Ellington later stated:

> I used to spend nights listening to Doc Perry,
> Louis Brown, and Louis Thomas. They were

schooled musicians who had been to the con-
servatory. But I listened to the unschooled, too.
There was a fusion, a borrowing of ideas, and
they helped one another right in front of where
I was standing, leaning over the piano, listening. Oh, I was a great listener![39]

Harlem Nocturne

As Duke Ellington finished his high school years, he was already
gaining recognition as a pianist and band leader. The pools and
bar rooms provided him a decent living, and temptations. Even
though he was a young man, he was already learning the under-
world of the music business, the connections between the music
industry and organized crime and the criminal syndicates that
underpinned the music industry.[40]

Even though DC was a great place to be mentored and to
learn from others, Ellington recognized that he needed to move
to another city to enhance his reputation. This was the time
of the Great Migration and Ellington recognized there were
greater opportunities for musicians in cities such as Harlem,
Atlantic City, and Chicago. These cities had a thriving music
scene, often bolstered by Prohibition.

Ellington and his musical peers, deciding to try out Harlem,
left DC. But without proper representation and support, Ellington and his band's first foray into the big city was unsuccessful.
All they could find were short-time gigs at rent parties. His son
Mercer later wrote that he "would always have someone walking around the after-hours spots like Mexico's at 133rd and

Lenox to tell them how important Duke Ellington was, what a rare artist he was, and how they would enjoy listening to him." In Harlem he "had begun to learn the art of hustling in back halls and dark alleys, how to play at top level in places that were prepared for 'sport.'"[41]

After Ellington's first efforts in Harlem failed, he returned home to DC. With so many artists out there and the growing importance of record deals and radio, the most successful musicians had to have proper representation. After regrouping, he and his band moved to Atlantic City. His musical breakthrough came when he hired Irving Mills as his producer and manager. Mills Music would buy songs and often retain the copyright by paying the author outright. Mills had the right connections, some legitimate and some less so.

The contract between the two men gave Mills roughly 50 percent of the royalties. While this may be considered extortion, the arrangement served Ellington well. Mills not only wanted Ellington to write songs, but he wanted Duke's band to play them. He marketed Ellington as a different type of Black performer, one who did not play up to racial stereotypes. Ellington's band presented themselves well, always dressed in suit and tie.

Perhaps most important of all, Mills got Duke Ellington and his band a full-time gig as the lead band at the Cotton Club, the most important club in all of Harlem. Run by gangsters and also serving as a speakeasy, the Cotton Club was an all-white club with Black performers. Only rarely were African Americans allowed into the club as patrons.

This was the height of the Harlem Renaissance, and many white people were beginning to recognize the artistic capabilities of African Americans. The Cotton Club attracted patrons like Carl Van Vechten, who was particularly interested in Black culture and a patron of Black arts. The performers and band played *jungle music*, a style that envisioned African Americans as somewhat primitive. While the dancers were scantily clad, light-skinned Black women, Ellington's band wore suits. Although the environment was certainly racist, the Cotton Club provided good exposure for its performers. The radio broadcast WHN took Ellington's music across the nation, and he and his band became one of the most popular groups.

While Ellington wrote his most popular songs during the period of his association with Irving Mills, Mills basically determined Duke's brand. It did not take long for Ellington to want to grow and demand greater control over his image and musical material. Furthermore, the death of his mother in 1935 and his father only two years later led him to question the direction of his life. In 1971, he wrote about this period:

> They [parents] left me such a heritage of belief that after they were gone it was natural I should turn to the Bible for help, again. I read it through four times. That took over two years. What did I get out of it? I thought that I knew something about life and living, about a good sound and grief and joy. But after studying the Scriptures, I found a new awareness of how to meet my problems, how to deal with my fellow man, and how to bring God further into my work.[42]

Ellington then wanted to write music that reflected his ancestry and his faith. In 1939, he fired Mills as manager and embarked on a new life of discovery.

Jump for Joy

In 1941, as the United States seemed on the path to war with the Axis Powers—Germany, Italy, and Japan—Ellington produced a new work titled *Jump for Joy,* a revue that consisted of music, dance, and theatrical performance. While some of Ellington's earlier work exhibited his pride in being African American, these messages had been subtle. Finally free from his management, Ellington could now pursue more edgy and race-conscious work. As the 1940s brought new conversations about race-relations nationwide, Ellington boldly made steps to enter that conversation.

Jump for Joy not only featured his band but it also included performers such as Dorothy Dandridge. When it opened at the Mayan Theater in Los Angeles, the edgy material most likely shocked those in attendance. Ellington saw this work as one that would break all the old stereotypes of African Americans and emancipate them. In an interview, Ellington stated his intentions for the play.

> The first and greatest problem is of trying to give an American audience entertainment without compromising the dignity of the Negro people. Needless to say, this is the problem every Negro artist faces. He runs afoul of offensive stereotypes, instilled in the

American mind by whole centuries of ridicule and derogation. The American audience has been taught to expect a Negro on the stage to clown and 'Uncle Tom,' that is, to enact the role of a servile, yet loveable inferior.[43]

The revue was a success. So much so, that it inspired Ellington to begin work on an even greater work. In 1943, he produced *Black, Brown, and Beige*. In this work, Ellington expanded on the themes of *Jump for Joy*. As he found his voice, he began to express his faith in stronger terms. When *Black, Brown, and Beige* was first performed at Carnegie Hall, Ellington not only brought the African American experience into the theater but he interpreted that experience as a spiritual journey.

With World War II now a reality and African Americans seeking a Double V (*victory over fascism* and *victory over racism*), *Black, Brown, and Beige* told the story of African Americans in three parts. *Black* was the period that African Americans came to America enslaved. This part of the story focuses heavily on their faith through a series of work songs and spirituals. He wrote and composed the lyrics to "Come Sunday," a song that expressed his own growing Christian faith. This song, recalling the spirituals of the previous century, represents Ellington's belief in God and the ways African Americans looked to the Lord for guidance throughout their trials both past and present.

The second part, *Brown*, explored life through the wars. It highlighted African American heroes of the Revolutionary War through the Buffalo Soldiers in the Spanish-American War. The final stage, *Beige*, examined World War I through the present. It incorporated the Harlem renaissance and the flowering of African American culture through the idiom of the *New Negro*.[44]

Jump for Joy and *Black, Brown, and Beige* laid the groundwork for Ellington's most important works, his three sacred concerts. In 1962, Ellington agreed to write a program of sacred music for the dedication of Grace Cathedral in San Francisco. The concert would be a worship service. With Ellington reaching the last stages of his life, he began to focus more on his faith. Ellington wrote, "I recognized this as an exceptional opportunity. Now I can say openly . . . what I have been saying to myself on my knees."[45] Indeed, the sacred concerts would be an expression of Ellington's faith, his relationship with God, and his confidence in the power of prayer.

As humans, we either place pressure on ourselves or feel pressure to be successful. The drive for success can become an addiction. Awards and recognitions feel good. At the same time, success often leaves us feeling empty if we are not working for something more important.

In the case of Duke Ellington, even though his career brought many accolades, he viewed his first sacred concert as the most important project he had ever done. For the concert, he wrote pieces such as "In the Beginning God," about God's majesty in creating the heavens and the earth. Another standout song was "Ninety-Nine Percent," about how we must give our all to God because 99 percent is not good enough.

Ellington's sacred concert was not a onetime event. He performed concerts throughout the United States, mostly in churches. Ellington even referred to himself as a messenger for the Lord.

I think of myself as a messenger boy, one who tries to bring messages to people, not people who have never heard of God, but those who were more or less raised with the guidance of the Church. Now and then we encounter people who say they do not believe. I hate to say that they are out and out liars, but I believe they think it fashionable to speak like that, having been brainwashed by someone beneath them, by someone with a complex who enjoys bringing them to their knees in the worship of the nonexistence of God. They snicker in the dark as they tremble with fright.[46]

In 1968 and 1973, he recorded new material for his second and third sacred concerts. In his second concert, there was an exuberance to the performances, encouraging Christians to look within themselves. Ellington's songs also explored the importance of prayer ("Meditation" and "Don't Get down on Your Knees to Pray until You Have Forgiven Everyone"); forgiveness ("Father Forgive"); and praise ("Praise God and Dance").

As Ellington entered the last years of his life, his spiritual music became a consolation. He viewed his relationship with God as his strength. His third recording of sacred music, not as well received by critics as the previous two, was perhaps his most introspective. Recorded less than a year before his death, as he struggled with lung cancer, Ellington embraced his mortality through his music.

One song, "The Majesty of God," expresses Ellington's looking forward to meeting God. Then there is "Ain't Nobody Nowhere Nothin' without God," which can be seen as expressing that, even though his body was ravaged with cancer, he was still someone because he was a believer. Another song inserted in the concert was the "The Lord's Prayer: My Love." Here Ellington explored the total majesty of God the Father.

Nearing his end, Ellington had embraced his faith. Finding his voice helped him to proclaim his faith publicly. He realized that his musical talent was a gift from God. In one of his last interviews, when a reporter asked him the reason for his success, he replied, "The grace of God." When the same interviewer tried to see if he believed in anything else, Ellington calmly replied, "How does one manage without God?"[47]

Conclusion

Thomas Dorsey, Ethel Waters, and Duke Ellington were three of the most important musicians of the twentieth century. The circumstances of their early lives led them to search for the truth. Their journeys also led them to dark periods in life. It is the same for us. Our past often presents barriers to our relationship with God. This is not because God does not love us, but because the memories of our past prevent us from seeing ourselves as candidates for grace and mercy and the label *children of God.*

As humans we are to live in the world, and certainly the world provides many pleasures. However, the Lord always speaks to us by calling us to a higher state of existence. Today Jesus is still calling us to follow Him with an unshakable faith: "Whoever wants to be my disciple must deny themselves and take up their cross and follow me" (Matthew 16:24). Until we do so, we will live unfulfilled lives. When we do make that decision, God will provide a peace that surpasses all understanding.

Explore Your Faith with Dorsey, Waters, and Ellington

* Dorsey, Waters, Ellington—all fought some form of depression or darkness in their lives. How can faith help us through dark periods in our lives?

* What is it about the world that keeps us from pursuing the path God has paved for us?

* When each of the persons profiled in this chapter left home, his or her faith was challenged at certain points. How do we respond when this happens in our lives?

CHAPTER 5

CHALLENGES, REDEMPTION, AND COMMUNITY

Fear not, for I have redeemed you; I have called you by name, you are mine. When you pass through the waters, I will be with you; and through the rivers, they shall not overwhelm you; when you walk through fire you shall not be burned, and the flame shall not consume you.

ISAIAH 43:1–2 ESV

God has not given us a spirit of fear (2 Timothy 1:7). Throughout our life's journey, we are confronted with many challenges. Our calling as Christians is not to the safe or easy path, for we know that Jesus said that, in actuality, we will be hated for our faith in Him. And, at the same time, we are not to feel depressed over the obstacles. Faith in God gives us the strength to rise up and stand against all sorts of obstacles.

Throughout history, this is the kind of unshakable faith that has sustained African Americans. The last chapter explored the ways that Black people found their voice in the era of Jim Crow. At the same time, we saw how the pressures of life include internal and external factors. Thomas Dorsey, Duke Ellington, and Ethel Waters all faced the horrors of Jim Crow, but at the same time, they found themselves conflicted internally. Racism was a problem—no doubt. However, life's issues extend, then and now, beyond racism.

As individuals, our struggles are the result of myriad issues. For much of my adult life, I have struggled with depression and anxiety. Being Black in America has been a large part of my struggle. It's simply hard to be Black in America. Period. It's hard to be a Black man in America. All too often we carry the burdens our ancestors never reconciled.

I didn't fit into the expectations of what a Black man should be. Not the stereotypical athlete, I was a music lover. I have had other issues, and had to learn how to accept myself for who I am. I didn't trust my voice; I didn't know if I had one. Twelve years ago, the situation became so bad that I briefly contemplated suicide. Little did I know that I suffered from clinical depression. I didn't have the words to understand what my emotions made me feel. What I did know was that those feelings brought me to a dark place.

In my journal that I kept during that period, I spoke of my life as a dark pit. Eventually, I sought medical help and was put on antidepressants, which I used for more than a year. I hated taking antidepressants because they made me feel numb to everything around me. However, to feel numb felt better at that time. With counseling, I slowly learned how to claim my voice.

One of the Scriptures I embraced is from Jonah. Swallowed in the belly of a great fish, Jonah also spoke of a dark place:

> In my distress I called to the LORD,
>> and he answered me.
> From deep in the realm of the dead I called for help,
>> and you listened to my cry.
> You hurled me into the depths,
>> into the very heart of the seas,
>> and the currents swirled about me;
> all your waves and breakers
>> swept over me.
> I said, "I have been banished
>> from your sight;
> yet I will look again
>> toward your holy temple."
> The engulfing waters threatened me,
>> the deep surrounded me;
>> seaweed was wrapped around my head.
> To the roots of the mountains I sank down;
>> the earth beneath barred me in forever.
> But you, LORD my God,
>> brought my life up from the pit. (Jonah 2:2–6)

God brought Jonah out from his dark place after he called on Him. I, too, learned to call on the Lord when I felt depressed. Reciting this Scripture helped me. I felt comforted and loved. I believed that soon I would be delivered too. Indeed, God did bring me out of the pit as well. Getting out of that pit was not easy. Over time, I began to rebuild the fractured pieces of my life. It was a difficult process that included many peaks and valleys. Some days I felt normal—other days I felt as if I were back in the pit.

When I was told that I could come off of the antidepressants gradually, I celebrated because I thought that I had overcome the worst part. Yet, weaning myself off medication did not go as I had expected. I did not realize I had developed a dependency on the medication. I experienced severe withdrawals. It was one of the most horrible experiences I've ever felt. I had no control over my emotions or feelings. Quickly, I went back to taking the full dose of the medication. Had I not done so I may have had a complete breakdown. I didn't give up and eventually was able to wean myself off the medication. That came with great difficulty.

Emerging from that place, I noticed that I had begun to reclaim the faith I had embraced as a young adult. I found my voice and a community to be a part of. I found me. My depression was also a spiritual condition and, securing my voice and my faith allowed me to gradually find freedom from bondage. I have not taken antidepressant medication since that time. I know that God has stood with me and carried me through the valley and across that plateau. While my story may be different from yours, I do know that God helps us in our darkest moments.

Changes on the Horizon

The African American community continually forges forward to move beyond the chambers of racial oppression. Overcoming obstacles includes much more than overcoming others' racism. We must also take steps to accept ourselves. The legacy of slavery led not only to discriminatory laws and customs but also to Black people thinking less of themselves. From holding to *colorism* prejudice about the darker shades of our skin tones, to detesting rather than adoring our kinkier hair textures, Black people have struggled, and continue to struggle, to accept and love ourselves the way that God made us. This is one of the saddest legacies of colonialism and slavery. Systemic racism is extremely difficult. It teaches hatred but can be overcome. However, hating oneself destroys everything.

The era of *Jim Crow*, the term that encompasses societal laws based on the segregation of the African American community, spanned from the end of Reconstruction to the passage of the Civil Rights Act of 1964 and the Voting Rights Act of 1965. The *Plessy v. Ferguson* Supreme Court decision in 1896 legally established "separate but equal" as an acceptable practice. For roughly the next forty years, Supreme Court cases such as *Cumming v. Richmond County Board of Education* strengthened the nation's parameters for legal and federally supported segregation.

Only in the late 1930s did the tide begin to turn. Much of the intellectual and moral credit has to go to Charles Hamilton Houston, a lawyer at Howard University who also worked as special counsel for the NAACP. Houston believed that the best way to overturn *Plessy* and to challenge segregation was to force localities to uphold the requirement of equal funding. As required in *Plessy*, segregated institutions had to be separate *and* equal. Houston knew that most—if not all—segregated institutions were not equal, and that this was appropriate grounds to challenge segregation.

In 1938, Houston was lead attorney arguing the *Missouri ex. rel. Gaines v. Canada* case before the Supreme Court. He argued that the state was in error in prohibiting Lloyd Gaines admission to the University of Missouri School of Law on the basis of race since no other law school existed in the state for African Americans. The Supreme Court decided in favor of Gaines, initiating a long period of reassessment of the *Plessy v. Ferguson* decision that culminated in the *Brown v. Board of Education* decision in 1954 that determined state laws supporting segregation in public schools were unconstitutional.

Bolstered by judicial decisions affirming their humanity, African Americans not only relied on the courts to pursue their rights. A new generation of leaders pursued civil rights in a number of ways. Particularly in the South, these activists took on tremendous risks to pursue their dreams. Fear of death was not the only risk, as the economic and social realities of life in Jim Crow America were devastating.

As African Americans transitioned into the Civil Rights era, they saw numerous changes. Nonetheless, leadership in the Black community remained linked to the church and the Christian community, meaning that the most powerful leaders of the movement drew their inspiration from their faith. Many Black churches and pastors did not fully embrace the struggle at the beginning; however, some did.

Vernon Johns, pastor of Dexter Avenue Baptist Church in Montgomery, Alabama, boldly preached about civil rights to his congregation, and Johns and others also offered their pulpits to other activists. Reverend Adam Clayton Powell Jr., pastor of Abyssinian Baptist Church, one of the oldest Black Churches in the United States, ran for congress in the state of New York and won on a platform of civil rights. Powell would remain a representative in congress from 1945 to 1971. Fred Shuttlesworth, pastor of Bethel Baptist Church, Birmingham, Alabama, was a founder of the Alabama Christian Movement for Human Rights and the Southern Christian Leadership Conference, two organizations instrumental in the Birmingham rights campaign of 1963.

The reason that faith was so important in the quest for African American civil rights was that African Americans saw their Christian faith as the *foundation* for their civil rights activism. Black people believed that Christ is on the side of justice and equality. They were not alone. Reverend Billy Graham was the most famous evangelist in America and perhaps the world and, by the late 1950s, had concluded that Christ and segregation and the discrimination that emerged as a result of it were incompatible.

The story of Black women over the first six decades of the twentieth century also demonstrates the ways that faith inspires people to press forward in spite of economic, physical, and psychological challenges. Black women took on the mantle of struggle to eradicate American hatred and oppression. Not surprisingly, many did so with the faith they learned from their communities that became rooted in their personal faith and life principles as Christians.

Mary McLeod Bethune: Missionary to the Race

Booker T. Washington inspired an entire generation of Black leaders. His advocacy of Black determination and his support for vocational training also inspired and helped many Black people. Mary McLeod Bethune (I will use her married name throughout for clarity) was perhaps the most important leader that Washington inspired. Like Washington, Bethune was from the rural South. Even though she was never a slave, almost all of her family had felt the pain of being owned by someone. Bethune's success is in large part a result of the fact that she experienced and responded to God's call to spread the gospel.

Bethune came to view education as an extension of Christian missionary work. In that capacity, Bethune wanted to transform society by providing access to education centered on Christian ethics and principles. In terms of her support for civil rights, Bethune sought out the Bible for her stand in opposition to segregation, and was willing to quote the Word as needed. Indeed, throughout her life she refused to budge on her push toward a more equitable society.

Bethune tirelessly worked on the behalf of numerous women's club organizations, including the National Association of Colored Women, where she served for many years as the chapter president of the Florida delegation. In this position, she helped organize Black women so that they could protest lynching and help register Black men and women to vote. Additionally, she demonstrated the importance of service. Even though she knew that she wanted to run her own school, she did not hesitate to work at other schools and was satisfied working with other people even if she wasn't in charge.

Bethune rose from humble beginnings as a cotton farmer in rural South Carolina to become the most powerful Black person in America during the 1930s. As she ascended to this position of prominence, she developed a close relationship to First Lady Eleanor Roosevelt and even served as a personal adviser to President Franklin Roosevelt. Toward the end of her life, she became involved in helping to prevent nuclear war as well as becoming one of the founders for the United Negro College Fund. She did all of this without compromising her Christian ethics.

Early Life

The fifteenth of seventeen children of Samuel and Patsy McLeod, Mary McLeod Bethune was born in 1875 in a poor, rural community in Mayesville, South Carolina. From her parents she learned about her family's experiences during slavery. She also learned how to handle the tough racial climate of a post-slave South. From Bethune's interviews later in her life, it appears that her parents were owned by two different masters. However, they lived in close proximity. Most of Bethune's siblings were born enslaved, and some of them were sold. Bethune later remarked that "some were scattered." They were grateful that none of the siblings were sold far from home. After slavery ended, the family was able to unite.[1]

While the McLeod's were poor and landless in their first years after emancipation, they were a stable family. Even though Bethune's parents were illiterate, they passed down their spiritual beliefs, and shared their faith with each of their children. Additionally they instilled a sense of self-pride in them. Bethune did not lament over her skin color or her stature. Bethune was a beautiful, proud Black woman who certainly inherited much of this pride from her mother, whom she later referred to as "one of those grand educated persons that did not have letters."[2]

Bethune also learned from her mother the power of forgiveness and love. Bethune later wrote about the impact of her mother's faith. At night when everyone was sleep, or when her mother thought they were, this was her time to pray to the Lord. Bethune often woke up at this time to see her mother praying.

> There she was, in the dark, on her knees. I knew the form kneeling in the moonlight which poured in upon her, sometimes beside her bed, sometimes beside a chair. She would ask God for faith, for strength, for love, for forgiveness, for knowledge, for food and clothing—not for herself but for her children and for all the poor people.[3]

These prayers Bethune witnessed had tremendous impact on her, including on her interpretation of race relations. Even though her family experienced tremendous obstacles while enslaved, Bethune's mother maintained contact with her former master's family. Maintaining these relationships should not be viewed in the context of trying to forget slavery or accepting the conditions of it. Rather, it was a sign of her mother's Christian heart. Bethune also saw from her mother that these relations could be beneficial. "My mother kept in rather close contact with the people she served as a slave. She continued to cook for her master until she [saved enough to purchase] five acres of land."[4] Even owning this small amount of land placed the family in a greater status because the majority of Black people in Mayesville did not own any land.[5]

Bethune's mother often brought her along when she did work at her former master's home. The interaction with her mother's former masters had a definitive impact on her life. She recalled on one occasion that she was in the yard playing with one of the children of her mother's former master. This did not make Mary feel inferior; but it challenged her. Bethune recognized that she could not read as the other child could, a fact that "just did something to my pride and my heart that made me feel that someday I would read just as she was reading."[6]

At the same time, Bethune treasured these struggles.

> Often, I thank God for my rugged ways. Have not my people come over a way that with tears has been watered? But we are stronger today through the struggles with overcoming. I am stronger today because as I have taken the steep, hard way, I have taken time to be faithful, preserving and hopeful.[7]

There were no schools in Mayesville for Black children, and the local white community did not support opening schools to educate former slaves. Bethune later stated that the white people in her community believed that Black people did not need education.[8] The reality, however, was much different. Education changed Bethune's life.

When she was roughly eight years old, the Presbyterian Church established a missionary school named Mayesville Institute.

Schools such as this relied heavily on contributions from northern philanthropists, people who had an interest in helping former slaves. Emma Wilson, the founder of the school, was an African American Presbyterian missionary who organized the school mostly through the assistance of northern philanthropists.

In many ways, Wilson's life mirrored Bethune's. Both women believed that Black people were equal and that with hard work they could achieve equality. Wilson was born a slave and first learned to read through the help of a white playmate on her master's farm. An excellent student, Wilson later attended Scotia Seminary on scholarship. Scotia Seminary was a Presbyterian school in North Carolina established in 1867 for Black women, to train them to go into missionary work.

Wilson was Bethune's first real mentor, and she encouraged her in her faith too. The school Bethune attended was small, including only "some home-made benches, a little table, and desks, a little pulpit, a little wood stove in the corner."[9] Many of Bethune's classmates came to class wearing rags. Indeed, a later report noted that the school had to clothe most of the students. At least Bethune had adequate clothing, and by this time, her family had become landowners.

As the first in her family to learn how to read and write, Bethune took pride in helping other family members learn how to read and write. Years later, Bethune spoke with pride about the fact that she was able to "read the newspapers and magazines and the Bible to them—that they had in their own home somebody who could do that—that was the greatest thrill."[10]

As an educated African American woman, Bethune understood the impact education had. While white residents where she lived did not support education for African Americans overall, Bethune noted that "it was remarkable the way [people] accepted me when I came back—how they used me to put down their figures for them." In her own life, education gave her opportunities that she would not have had without it. Even on farms, Bethune argued, educated African Americans got better jobs. "It seemed then that every Negro boy and girl who could read and write could be of great service on the farm."[11]

Bethune attended the Trinity Presbyterian Church located at the Mayesville Institute. She also attended Sunday school. At graduation, Bethune professed her faith "before the elders of the church to be questioned as to her religious [tenets]—her belief in God and in eternal salvation."[12] At this point, Bethune joined Trinity Presbyterian Church.

Although Bethune had found her religious calling by the time she had graduated from Mayesville Institute, there was little opportunity for a Black woman to continue her education where she lived. It was back to the cotton fields. Disappointed by the situation but not dismayed, Bethune waited for an opportunity. She later stated that she "did all I could in the community to keep alive the interest in education, keeping up intercession for opportunity to train myself that I might be of service to others."[13]

Sadly, many people see their dreams dashed because of a lack of opportunity. Bethune's story offers hope but is also a call to those in positions of influence to provide opportunities to those in need. At the same time, Bethune remained patient, knowing that God had plans for her. "I feel [God] working in and through me, and I have learned to give myself—freely—unreservedly to the guidance of the inner voice in me."[14]

Bethune's faith that God would provide a way out of Mayesville was soon confirmed. While Bethune returned to the cotton fields after school and prayed to God for an opportunity, another woman halfway across the nation read stories about Presbyterian missions to Southern African Americans. Mary Chrisman read a report about the Mayesville Institute in a Presbyterian journal. The story highlighted the impact education had on the young students. It inspired her so much that she decided to sponsor a student from the Mayesville Institute to attend Scotia Seminary in North Carolina.

Chrisman, a white woman who lived in Denver, Colorado, wrote a letter to Emma Wilson. Wilson immediately thought that Bethune would be the perfect candidate for the scholarship. Thrilled about the opportunity, Wilson rushed to Bethune's home to offer her the opportunity. As she approached the farm, she saw all of the family, including Mary, working in the cotton fields.

Wilson first spoke to Bethune's parents to see if they would accept the scholarship. Bethune's mother was excited because

"I FEEL [GOD] WORKING IN AND THROUGH ME, AND I HAVE LEARNED TO GIVE MYSELF—FREELY—UNRESERVEDLY TO THE GUIDANCE OF THE INNER VOICE IN ME."
—MARY MCLEOD BETHUNE

she knew that this was her daughter's ticket out of the cotton fields. Tears giving glory to God dripped from her eyes as she understood that this was her daughter's choice, whether or not she would take this opportunity. Looking at her daughter and her other children in the background, she asked her daughter if she wanted to accept the opportunity to attend Scotia Seminary.

Bethune thought about the opportunity, knowing that it meant leaving her home and family. But she realized that this was God's will for her life. She yelled yes and later said that she "pulled my cotton sack off, got down on my knees, clasped my hands, and turned my eyes upward and thanked God for the chance that had come.[15]

As a student at Scotia, Bethune had access to some of the most committed Christian female missionaries in the country. These women not only encouraged her spiritually but also encouraged her to have even more confidence. The Black teachers helped Bethune. They trained her in proper etiquette and helped her to dream even greater. Through the mentorship of these women, Bethune gained confidence in her abilities and her future.[16]

As Bethune was surrounded by missionaries, her desire to become a missionary after graduation isn't surprising. To do so, however, required even more education. With the support of another benefactor, she entered the May Institute in Chicago, an institution that would later become the Moody Bible Institute, named after its founder Dwight (D. L.) Moody. At the May Institute, Bethune interacted freely with D. L. Moody and credited him with having a major impact on her journey.

Moody, a successful businessman, gave up this life in order to become an evangelist. Meeting and learning from someone dedicated to forgoing a prominent lifestyle in order to preach God's Word had an impact on the young Bethune. Bethune was already ecumenical and evangelical in her religious worldview and comfortable in many different Christian traditions. The May Institute only furthered Bethune's desire to become a missionary in Africa. This dream was unattainable, however.

When Bethune applied to the Bible Institute for Home and Foreign Missions for a position as a missionary in Africa, the missions board informed her that they did not have any positions for African Americans at that time.[17] While Bethune was disappointed, her faith caused her to view it as God's will. Bethune then decided to focus on the plight of African Americans in the South.

God always opens doors when others close them.

Toward Bethune-Cookman College: A Christian Mission

When I think about Mary McLeod Bethune and her life, I am reminded of King Jehu and his devotion to the things he was passionate about: "'Come with me and see my zeal for the Lord.' Then he had him ride along in his chariot" (2 Kings 10:16). The Bible tells us that Jehu, upon receiving his commission from the Lord, had tremendous zeal. The Bible reiterates this man's passion by saying that he drove his chariot like a "maniac" (9:20). His passion for the Lord imbued everything he did. Jehu's zeal meant that he was undeterred by the obstacles he faced.

Mary McLeod Bethune had a zeal and passion for the Lord and helping her community. Inspired by men and women who felt likewise, Bethune entered a life of service with the same passion that had inspired and helped her in difficult times. Though disappointed that she would not receive an appointment to be a missionary in Africa, she was undeterred by this setback and kept pressing forward. The obstacles ironically helped her craft the values for her missions work. Refusing to give up and trusting in the Lord, she would establish part of her legacy—an institution that would become Bethune-Cookman College.

Since her youth, Bethune believed that God had called her to educate the "least of these." Though she initially thought that this would lead her to Africa, after graduating from the May Institute after two years and learning that there was not a position for her, she turned her attention to the Southern United States. First, she accepted a position at a school in Augusta, Georgia, to work with a woman named Lucy Laney.

Laney was the founder of the Haines Institute, a school for Black children in Augusta. Started in the basement of the church Laney attended, the school had grown in the years before Bethune arrived. For Bethune, Laney was another Black woman God placed in front of her as a mentor. She was able to see that Black women were changing the world and transforming their communities. Such mentorship inspired Bethune tremendously.[18]

> "COME WITH ME AND SEE MY ZEAL FOR THE LORD."
> THEN HE HAD HIM RIDE ALONG IN HIS CHARIOT.
> (2 KINGS 10:16)

Indeed, we often dismiss how important it is to have mentors and leaders who look like us or have had similar experiences. These men and women inspire us because they give us hope that if they could—we can too. I know in my life how grateful I am for all my mentors, from all backgrounds. Those who have had a similar background have filled a very special role and have had a great impact on my life.

The work Bethune did during these early years encouraged her to focus on the value of Black uplift and self-determination. Bethune realized that Black people needed examples of Black success and excellence in order to boost their self-image. At the same time, she believed that this needed to be undergirded by Christian values. Although Bethune was only at the Haines Institute for one year, she accomplished much more than teaching classes. Wanting to do more work in the community, she opened her own Sunday school.

Bethune recognized that there were many people living around the institute, many who were unable to attend school. Therefore, Bethune asked Laney if she could start a mission Sunday school at the Haines Institute. The Sunday school was opened to more than the students attending the school; Bethune recruited the girls from the science class and her own class and "went out and combed the alleys and streets and brought in hundreds of children until we had a Sunday school of almost a thousand young people and people in the community came in."[19] Even after she left Haines, the mission Sunday school she started lasted many years, a fact Bethune was proud of and highlighted decades later.[20]

From Haines Institute, Bethune moved back to South Carolina to work at the Kendall Institute. This school was located in Sumter, South Carolina, and was led by Reverend C. J. Watkins. Bethune also saw this school as a platform from which to spread the gospel. Again, her ministry extended beyond the school walls. She stated that the school was "another field for real service, never tiring."[21] Bethune worked hard, setting up meetings with numerous people in the community, from farmers to incarcerated people. After building relationships with many in the community, she knew what the people wanted. Through these conversations, she decided to open a Sunday school and organize community meetings.

It was in the church connected with the institute that she met Albertus Bethune, who would soon become her husband. Bethune and her husband would have one child.

Bethune's travels next took her to Palatka, Florida, in 1899. Five years later, she moved to Daytona Beach, Florida, where she would finally establish the school she believed that God had been preparing her for through her past experiences. She named the school the Daytona Educational and Industrial Training School For Negro Girls. In 1923, the school merged with Cookman Institute, a co-ed institution affiliated with the Methodist Church. In 1931, the institution officially became Bethune-Cookman College. Bethune served as president of the college until she retired in 1942.[22]

Bethune had only $1.50 when she arrived in Daytona from Palatka. Without much money, she had to find a place to rent for the school. She was able to find a place, but still had to build a school. She hired local carpenters and farmers who helped to build the school and provide food for the students and faculty. The same farmers helped the school plant a garden so that the students could raise vegetables and fruit, then sell them in order to help raise funds for the school.[23]

Even with the help of the community, the school had problems providing for its staff and students. Bethune often spoke about one experience during the early years, when the school was in so much debt that it did not have enough money to feed the people on campus. The situation was so grave that most people had given up. But Bethune had faith God would provide. With people starving and worried about what was to become of the school, Bethune stood up and prayed for God to help them. After prayer, Bethune encouraged others on the campus to sing hymns and pray. The whole building was praying and singing praises to God. As they were praying, "a man drove up in his wagon with a load of vegetables and potatoes and food stuff that a friend had sent over." God answered their prayers right then. One of the girls said, "Mrs. Bethune prayed for food and here is a man with a wagon full."[24]

The school was in need of constant repair. Without the luxury of an endowment, though, any necessary upkeep presented a problem. When a roof needed to be mended immediately, Bethune didn't have the funds to fix it. She asked locals for help, but no one was able to. Without options, she had only her faith. She told one of the architects at the school, "Build scaffolding around the house. We have enough lumber for scaffolding."

Bethune's request stunned the carpenter who asked why they should build scaffolding when they did not yet have materials to fix the roof. Bethune did not relent and, relying on her faith, once again told the carpenter to "Build the scaffolds and get ready." That day she received a check for

$1,000 from an unexpected source. Bethune called everyone together, and "we bowed in prayer there together, thanking God for the supply."[25]

Mary McLeod Bethune was a woman of unshakable faith, who believed that her school was a Christian mission. She said, "That affirmation with God took me from the cotton fields to the little mission school to Scotia College to Moody Bible Institute, and finally, to the planting of the Bethune-Cookman College—the real child of my desire."[26]

Around the time of the union between the Methodist Church school and Bethune's institution, Bethune became a member of the Methodist Episcopal Church. Bethune wanted her school to be founded on the principles of vocational, liberal, and Christian ethics. In this manner, she sought to educate the entire student and to prepare them for lives of purpose, service, and leadership. Reflecting Bethune's ethics, the 1910 school catalogue stated:

> The aim of the institution is to uplift Negro girls spiritually, morally, intellectually, and industrially. The school stands for a broad, thorough practical training. To develop Christian character, to send forth women who will be rounded home-makers and Christian leaders is the aim of its founder and supporters; a trained mind, heart and hand being the idea of a complete education.[27]

Preparing for the Future

Bethune's faith inspired her to seek out and to work with people of different backgrounds. Her political savvy took her to numerous organizations and countries. She wrote that when "hatred has been projected toward me, I have known that the persons who extended it lacked spiritual understanding." Bethune wrote, "I have had great pity and compassion on them. Our Heavenly Father pitieth each one of us when we fail to understand. Jesus said of those who crucified him: Father forgive them, for they do not know what they do."[28]

Bethune's life encourages me to aspire to love my enemies without limits. Through her love and strength, her life demonstrates that there is power in prayer. God is able to take anyone and use them for His will. Loving the people who may not love us back, or who work against us, is difficult. However, we are called by God to this work. For those of us interested in the work of reconciliation, love is the solution. Bethune's success in reconciliation came as a result of her commitment to loving everyone and to dialogue.

> Never be lacking in zeal, but keep your spiritual fervor, serving the Lord. Be joyful in hope, patient in affliction, faithful in prayer. Share with the Lord's people who are in need. Practice hospitality" (Romans 12:11–13).

The Voice and Conscience of the Civil Rights Movement: Fannie Lou Hamer

Although some historians speak about the existence of a long civil rights movement that extends from emancipation to today, one could argue that the struggle for equality has been an issue

> NEVER BE LACKING IN ZEAL, BUT KEEP YOUR SPIRITUAL FERVOR, SERVING THE LORD. BE JOYFUL IN HOPE, PATIENT IN AFFLICTION, FAITHFUL IN PRAYER. SHARE WITH THE LORD'S PEOPLE WHO ARE IN NEED. PRACTICE HOSPITALITY.
> (ROMANS 12:11–13)

since 1619. There were specific issues and a narrative context that make the period from 1954 through 1968 worthy to be set apart, and I prefer the chronology for the African American civil rights movement occurring between 1954 and 1968.

The beginning of the African American civil rights movement was in 1954 with the *Brown v. Board of Education* decision. *Brown* was the culmination of a series of Supreme Court cases that gradually dismantled segregation in our nation's schools. The next year several other major events gave energy to supporters and opponents of civil rights.

Because many school districts refused to desegregate their schools, the Brown case was once again brought before the Supreme Court. Just one year after its landmark decision in the first Brown case, the same court decided, in what is often called the *Brown II* decision, that schools had to integrate with "all deliberate speed." The court's insertion of integration in "all deliberate speed" sadly gave leeway for local districts to delay school integration.

This extended the period of integration until the *Green v. County School Board of New Kent County* case in 1968 that finally ended the last vestige of county-supported segregation. It did so when it struck down "freedom-of-choice" options. In order to appear to comply with the Brown decisions while maintaining segregation, many school systems offered the "opportunity" for parents to choose which school (white or Black) they wanted their child to attend. The *Alexander v. Holmes County Board of Education* decision in 1969 then ordered immediate desegregation of public schools.

In December 1955, police arrested Rosa Parks for refusing to give up her seat on a bus in Montgomery, Alabama. Although other African Americans had been arrested on the same city buses earlier, the African American community had finally had enough. A few days after Parks's arrest, Black women, led by Jo Ann Robinson, garnered support for a citywide boycott of buses in Montgomery.

The actions of Black women such as Parks and Robinson were the catalyst for the Montgomery Bus Boycott. The boycott extended from December 1955 to December 1956. During this period, Martin Luther King Jr., pastor at Dexter Avenue Baptist Church in Montgomery, emerged as a leader. Out of the Montgomery Bus Boycotts, the Southern Christian Leadership Conference (SCLC), an organization that would promote African American civil rights through nonviolence, was established. Martin Luther King Jr. would become the first president.

When many of us think about the civil rights movement, all too often we focus only on the Black male leaders like Martin Luther King Jr., C. K. Steele, and Ralph Abernathy. We often forget the important role of women who were the backbone of the movement, like Rosa Parks, Jo Ann Robinson, Ella Baker, Septima Poinsette Clark, and Mamie Till. While Black men typically led the major organizations of the movement —organizations such as the NAACP and SCLC, along with the Student Nonviolent Coordinating Committee (SNCC) and the Congress of Racial Equality (CORE)—Black women supported the movement in similarly important ways.

For example, Mamie Till's decision to open the casket of her son enabled the entire world to see what racism and hatred had led people to do to her son, Emmett. One can only imagine the pain of a mother to open that casket as if she were opening the emotional wounds inflicted on her in his tragic lynching. The pictures taken at the funeral were published in *Jet* magazine for everyone to see. Her decision provided so much inspiration and strength to the movement at a tremendous psychological cost to herself.

Even though Black women were often the movement's backbone and conscience, their contributions have often been overlooked. In doing so, we negate the movement's spiritual underpinnings. As it is to this day, Black women comprise the majority of African American churchgoers. Ella Baker, another prominent community organizer during the movement, later remarked, "The movement of the fifties and sixties was carried largely by women, since it came out of church . . . The number of women who carried the movement was much larger than that of men."[29]

As devout Black women sustained, nurtured, and propelled the movement, the Black Church became the movement's sanctuary. Black churches had been places of organization for generations. As Black people lived through the civil rights movement, the churchgoers saw the Church move more closely toward a prophetic purpose. Visible progress supported by the actions of fellow believers led even more Black people to realize that the Church remained a space where Black people believed that God was still working for them.

Not since the antebellum and civil war eras did the Black Church take on such a prophetic role. The movement reinvigorated the traditional spirituals and work songs of African Americans. Songs such as "Oh, Freedom" were sung alongside the more recent Black gospel songs such as "Precious Lord, Take My Hand," making the churches and the songs even more relevant.

The average civil rights worker was a poor Black churchgoer who had experienced firsthand the trauma of racial oppression. While Black women were largely barred from pulpit ministry, the Church did offer them a voice. In Black churches, women played the music and sang in the choirs. Black women prayed with Black men for liberation. Black women were the church secretaries. The feel of the civil rights movement, when you evaluate it, was that of the essence of the power of the Black Church.

Few people during the African American civil rights movement had a more powerful voice than Fannie Lou Hamer. Hamer is perhaps best known for her work with the Student Nonviolent Coordinating Committee (SNCC) and the Mississippi Freedom Democratic Party (MFDP), as well as her powerful testimony broadcast before the entire nation at the 1964 Democratic National Convention.

THE FEEL OF THE CIVIL RIGHTS MOVEMENT, WHEN YOU EVALUATE IT, WAS THAT OF THE ESSENCE OF THE POWER OF THE BLACK CHURCH.

Hamer was one of the founders of the MFDP, an organization formed to directly challenge Mississippi's all-white Democratic primary. As a representative of the MFDP, Hamer came to Atlantic City in 1964, the location of that year's Democratic National Convention, to protest Mississippi's all white democratic primary. In her testimony before the credentials committee, Hamer detailed her incarceration for trying to register to vote.

She also demanded that the Democratic Party remove Mississippi's delegates and seat the delegates from the Mississippi Freedom Democratic Party. Hamer's speech bothered President Lyndon Johnson so much that he hastily set up his own press conference to get her testimony from being broadcast across the nation. Johnson's attempts failed and news stations played recordings of the speech on the nightly news.

Hamer later ran for congress several times unsuccessfully and worked diligently in the antiwar and labor movements. Toward the end of her life, Hamer tried to bring poor workers of all backgrounds into cooperatives. She also founded the Freedom Farm Cooperative in 1969. With funds from outside sources, the cooperative purchased land so that farmers could buy into the cooperative. The people who bought into the cooperative would farm the land and would receive the proceeds from it.

Finally, remembering the horrors of her sterilization, the circumstances of which will be discussed later in this chapter, and arising from her deeply rooted Christian faith, Hamer became a strong opponent of abortion.[30]

Hamer's life demonstrates how hard life was for Black women living during the era of Jim Crow. As a Black person, she endured all of the consequences of her race. As a woman, she had to deal with sexism and misogyny. As a Black woman, she dealt with the consequences of her dual identities. Nevertheless, her passion, her faith, and her experiences can be classified as the moral compass of the entire movement. As an orator, her speeches were just as powerful as Martin Luther King's, perhaps more powerful for some listeners. Her power came from her own experiences.

Humble Beginnings

While many of the recognized leaders of the civil rights movement came from middle-class backgrounds, Fannie Lou Hamer did not. She was the last child of twenty in a family of sharecroppers who lived in Ruleville, Mississippi. Ruleville is a small town in Sunflower County, Mississippi. Sunflower County, part of western Mississippi, lies directly within the Mississippi Delta.

Hamer's early life in Ruleville was difficult to say the least. Mississippi was a state filled with tremendous racial contrasts. Much of Mississippi, particularly the Delta region, remained in a state of agricultural feudalism. A majority of African Americans in Mississippi continued to live in rural areas, with many living in a state of agricultural peonage (sharecropping, tenant farming, and other types of farm labor). A Black person's life had little value in the Delta as organizations like the Ku Klux Klan and the White Citizens' Council dominated the political and legal landscape. Rape and police brutality were commonplace.

Hamer's reflections on her early life raise the question about just how much had actually changed in the lives of Black people born in the Mississippi Delta since the end of slavery. Mississippi's educational system followed the same pattern of political and legal domination by white people. Black schools often received 10 to 25 percent of the funding that white schools received, if that. Because of a lack of funding, the grueling work expectations on the plantations, and the threat of violence, the dropout rate in Mississippi was strikingly high.[31]

Black Mississippians still lived on plantations under the control of white people one hundred years after the end of slavery. They were not totally free because, as sharecroppers, they had to pay debts to the plantation owner at the end of the year, a reality that often placed them in debt after an entire year of work. If they were unable to pay the debt, it advanced to the next year. The sharecropping system of lifelong debt bondage ensnared Hamer at an early age.

As a young girl of six, the plantation owner approached her one day upon learning her age to tell her that it was time for her to pick cotton. He made another arrangement with her. As a worker, she could purchase things that she liked from the plantation store on commission, he said. Specifically, he encouraged her to buy crackerjacks and sardines. Of course, none of these items were free. They were not even wholesale.

That day when Hamer was six, the plantation owner not only forced her into backbreaking work picking cotton, but he also lured the child into a lifelong state of indebtedness to owners like him. As Hamer would only later discover: The crushing power of debt undergirded the entire sharecropping system. Though she lived in twentieth-century America, Hamer's life resembled more that of a slave than a free person.[32]

Many plantation owners wanted Black families who worked for them to have children. Some plantation owners paid women workers money, often roughly $50, to have children. Plantation owners wanted sharecroppers to have children because it provided additional future field hands.[33] This is likely to have happened in the case of Hamer's family.

Ironically, while plantation owners wanted Black people to have children, many other white residents of Mississippi did not. At the local hospitals that would treat African Americans, doctors often performed illegal sterilizations on Black women to prevent them from having children. This happened to Hamer when she was given a hysterectomy against her knowledge at the local hospital in 1961.

Coming Out of the Darkness

How did Hamer—someone with only a sixth-grade education and who was working to survive as a sharecropper in Mississippi—become one of the most important leaders of the African American civil rights movement? The answer lies in Hamer's faith and her innate ability to express her emotions. Since her youth, the church had been the one place where Hamer found relief. The church was the one place that a Black woman with a sixth-grade education in Mississippi could gain recognition for her gifts.

The book of Isaiah says, "For I am the LORD your God who takes hold of your right hand and says to you, Do not fear; I will help you" (41:13). Church members helped cultivate Hamer's singing voice along with her exceptional oratory skills. From her youth she attended Baptist churches and was baptized at the Strangers Home Baptist Church.[34] Hamer believed that God was active in her life and that He was working through her. She also believed that God had a mission for her.

Other events helped to bring Hamer into the national spotlight. By 1962, members of SNCC, the group that had organized the student-led protests of segregated lunch counters throughout the South, had arrived in Mississippi. Under the leadership of Robert Moses, SNCC focused on voter registration in Mississippi. The state by this time had the most draconian policies of any state in the nation, effectively preventing the Black population from voting.

These policies included poll taxes, literacy tests, and intimidation. Intimidation included but was not limited to threats of firing Blacks who tried to register to vote. Local hate groups threatened, shot at, and even killed people in Mississippi for even daring to register to vote. For example, Herbert Lee, a

> FOR I AM THE LORD YOUR GOD WHO TAKES
> HOLD OF YOUR RIGHT HAND AND SAYS TO YOU,
> DO NOT FEAR; I WILL HELP YOU. (ISAIAH 41:13)

Black farmer who attempted to register in Amite County, was assassinated in 1961. Three years later, members of the KKK murdered activists James Chaney, Andrew Goodman, and Michael Schwerner, who were working with Robert Moses to promote voting rights, only 125 miles from Hamer's hometown.

The combination of intimidation and legal restrictions was so successful that in 1962, out of 422,256 Blacks who were eligible to vote in the state, only 21,209 were registered. Even many of those who did register to vote never voted—out of fear.[35] Mississippi's situation was so bad that Robert Moses decided to bring together all of the civil rights organizations in the state into an umbrella group he called the Council of Federated Organizations (COFO). Moses and other leaders believed that by working together and pooling their resources, they could make progress in voter registration or force the United States Justice Department to intervene on their behalf.

SNCC, now working through COFO, rededicated itself to organizing African Americans to try to get them to register. Local residents were willing to take the risk to support SNCC and COFO, and they opened their churches as spaces to organize. Even though the Klan and citizens councils demonstrated that they were willing to burn or bomb churches, church buildings were still safer meeting places than stores or people's homes. Word quickly spread through the Delta, and in 1962, SNCC representatives were in Sunflower County attempting to register voters.

At one of those meetings at William Chapel Missionary Baptist Church, SNCC organizers met Hamer. Hamer, the sharecropper who did not know her rights, sat in the church and felt a sense of hope rising up within her. She wanted to be an American citizen with rights and privileges. As she sat in the church and listened, she was convinced she did have a constitutional right to vote. At the same time, we should not limit Hamer's interest in civil rights to only social justice. Hamer believed her newfound passion was what God wanted her to fight for.

Hamer realized that while the SNCC activists who came to Mississippi had more education than she did, she was just as important as they were. Certainly, her faith helped her overcome her internal feelings of insecurity. In Isaiah, the prophet says:

> The Spirit of the Lord is on me,
>> because he has anointed me
>> to proclaim good news to the poor.
> He has sent me to proclaim freedom for the
>> prisoners
>> and recovery of sight for the blind,
> to set the oppressed free. (Luke 4:18)

Even before James Cone published his seminal work *Black Theology and Black Power* that defined Black Liberation Theology, Hamer expressed her belief that God was active in the liberation of Black people. At the same time, Hamer held to a literal interpretation of the Bible. She believed that God is not a respecter of persons. Therefore, God does not examine people by race or ethnicity: a fact that eventually led her to disagree with the growing radicalism of SNCC during the later period of the 1960s. Toward the end of her life, as she considered the path of civil rights, she reflected on Acts 17:26, and commented: "Whether he's white as a sheet or Black as a skillet, out of one

> **THE SPIRIT OF THE LORD IS ON ME, BECAUSE HE HAS ANOINTED ME TO PROCLAIM GOOD NEWS TO THE POOR. HE HAS SENT ME TO PROCLAIM FREEDOM FOR THE PRISONERS AND RECOVERY OF SIGHT FOR THE BLIND, TO SET THE OPPRESSED FREE. (LUKE 4:18)**

blood God made all nations."[36] Hamer was for the oppressed, regardless of their ethnicity. Her commitment to the entire body of Christ is instructive. All people in need, according to Hamer, needed to be elevated.

National Spotlight

Local SNCC organizers helped Hamer cultivate her talents and find her voice. She decided then that she wanted to register to vote. With their support, she along with a group of other Mississippi residents traveled almost seventy miles to Indianola, Mississippi, to attempt to register to vote. But when she got home, the owner of the plantation she lived on visited her home. He heard that Hamer had tried to register.

Standing at the door of her home located on his property, he told her she was wrong to try and that she had to get out of her home that night. Drawing on her strength and faith, Hamer responded to the owner of the property she lived on that "I didn't try to register for you. I tried to register for myself."

Hamer's husband could not leave because of the harvest.[37]

Hamer could not be deterred as she was convinced that this was God's work. And like slaves of a former generation, she relied on the story of the exodus to explain the conditions of people like her in Mississippi.

> You see the point is about this, and you can't deny it, not either one of you here in this room— not Negroes—we have prayed for change in the state of Mississippi for years. And God made it so plain He sent Moses down in Egypt-land to tell Pharaoh to let my people go. And He made it so plain here in Mississippi the man that heads the project is named Moses, Bob Moses. And he sent Bob Moses down in Mississippi, to tell all of these hate groups to let my people go.[38]

Hamer tried again to register to vote in 1963, and this time she passed the literacy test. While one might think that this was the end of the problem, local authorities then informed her that she needed to pay the poll tax. Frustrated but not deterred, Hamer continued working with SNCC activists. One day while she was traveling between South Carolina and Mississippi, police arrested Hamer and other members of her caravan in Winona, Mississippi, on fraudulent charges.

For the rest of her life, Hamer recounted the horrifying event. When she was in the holding center, she recalled, "I began to hear sounds of licks and screams. I could hear the sounds of licks and horrible screams. And I could hear somebody say, 'Can you say, yes, sir, nigger? Can you say yes, sir?' And they would say other horrible names."[39] Soon the prison guards came for Hamer.

> And it wasn't too long before three white men came to my cell. One of these men was a state highway patrolman and he asked me where I was from. And I told him Ruleville and he said, "We are going to check this." And they left my cell and it wasn't too long before they came back. He said, "You's from Ruleville all right," and he used a curse word. And he said, "We are going to make you wish you was dead."[40]

The state highway patrolman placed Hamer in a room where five men were—two Black men and three white men. One of the officers then gave a billy club to the Black prisoner and ordered him to beat Hamer. Hamer stated that the blackjack was "a long leather black jack and it was loaded with something heavy."[41] The first prisoner beat Hamer until he was exhausted. Then the same officer ordered that the second prisoner take the blackjack and continue the assault. During the second assault, the beating was so bad that her dress moved upward exposing Hamer's body. The beating soon turned into a full-blown sexual assault.[42]

During the assault, Hamer prayed to God, but she did not resist. There was nothing she could do but "scream and call on God."[43] The assault was so bad that she passed out after it was over. When she came to, she was unable to walk on her own. Battered, bruised, and assaulted so badly that she suffered physically for the rest of her life, Hamer still found the power to praise God for giving her the strength to survive. She also prayed for the people who assaulted her. This was the epitome of tough faith. From this moment, Hamer said that she prayed every night for her oppressors. "We are fighting to save these people from their hate and from all the things that would be so bad against them."[44]

Defending the Powerless

Hamer never relented in fighting for the less fortunate. Her cofounding of the MFDP catapulted her to fame, making her a universally recognized leader of the civil rights movement, but her advocacy brought her few comforts. She and her husband adopted two young girls, but Hamer sadly had to see one of them die. Her daughter Dorothy died in childbirth when she began hemorrhaging, and Hamer was unable to get a doctor to see her.[45]

Today when many people think about Hamer, they imagine her as an old woman. The truth is far from this. Hamer only spent fifteen years in the spotlight. Thrust into it in 1962, she died in 1977. She lived in a very small home when she died. Her body was much older than a person of only fifty-nine years.

When Hamer died, she suffered from a combination of heart disease, breast cancer, diabetes, and kidney damage. The kidney damage she suffered was a consequence of the beating she had endured in prison in 1963. Being Black in American contributed directly to her early death.

Even today, studies show that we often see Black girls as older and less innocent than other young girls. Their innocence of youth is stripped too early.[46]

Explore Your Faith with Mary McLeod Bethune and Fannie Lou Hamer

* How was Bethune attuned to the direction that God wanted her to go? What can we learn from her about hearing and following God's call?

* What does Hamer's life say about the power of forgiveness and universal love even to our oppressors?

* What does Hamer's life tell us about the need to speak for those who do not have a voice? Who are those people today?

CHAPTER 6

REFLECTIONS, PRAYERS FOR HEALING, AND A FINAL DEVOTION

*I press on toward the goal to win
the prize for which God has called
me heavenward in Christ Jesus.*

PHILIPPIANS 3:14

As a historian, one of the things I have come to realize is that life is a process. Throughout history, time unfolds one page at a time. At the same time, as we historians like to say, history often repeats itself. From politics to social issues, almost all of the issues we currently face have happened before. While the names, faces, and the groups involved change—our values, mistakes, prejudices, hopes, and dreams that have led to our present conditions have all too often remained unchanged. When we look at life through the prism of history, one wonders how much different humans are today than the historical Adam and Eve. The pressures they faced eventually led to their fall. Were they so different from us, and were their struggles so unlike what we feel or face today? I doubt it.

Reflections

What has not changed through time is the revelation of God to us through Jesus Christ. As Christians, we are saved and redeemed by His blood. That redemption, however, does not necessarily make our lives in this world easier. The flesh, that part of us so human and fragile, challenges every step of our journey.

Those of us who are interested in racial reconciliation must remain steadfast. In a polarized society, we must resist the temptation to segregate ourselves, and work to have more empathy and understanding. This is difficult work. We must press toward more dialogue and more understanding, and equity, across racial and ethnic boundaries. These conversations are destined to be difficult. However, that is another blessing of having unshakable faith. The current struggle over racial justice desperately needs Christian voices at the forefront.

Being a committed Christian is not an easy task in our society. The dialogue that is necessary is made difficult by modern realities. At almost every turn, we are asked to, sometimes demanded, to choose the world over our faith and our values. I suspect many Christians no longer believe that our faith is a solution, as the consequences for not bending to the world's way can be tremendous. Yet, as I think about it, it must have been difficult for Lott Cary and William Crane to collaborate as well. But they did it. They found the strength to break down the walls between them because they loved each other as Christian brothers.

The 24-hour information cycle can have a negative impact on our Christian walk. It's hard to hold firm when it seems every day we are fed stories about the decline of Christianity and faith in general. While some people seem to believe this is a conspiracy to ridicule people of faith, I believe it is an actual consequence of just how available news and information are to everyone. We are constantly bombarded. It's everywhere. We're tied to our computers and mobile gadgets. Information overload often makes it difficult to spend quality time reading and studying our Bibles and spending quality time with our Lord.

While the stories of people leaving the faith are often true, the 24-hour news cycle (and the easy access to it) likely makes these issues seem much more pervasive than they are.[1] Perhaps, we need greater perspective when we consider the role our faith continues to have in society. For centuries, individuals have predicted Christianity's demise and that of religion in general.

In 1822, Thomas Jefferson wrote that "I confidently expect that the present generation will see Unitarianism become the general religion of the United States."[2] In making his prediction, Jefferson expected Americans to abandon evangelical and mainstream Christianity altogether and to adopt a type of religion that was more *theist* and less *Christian*. Jefferson, one of our greatest thinkers, believed that Americans would abandon traditional Christianity, which upholds miracles, the Trinity, and the Resurrection.

History has proven Jefferson wrong. In his lifetime, even as he wrote his letter, he missed the great revival happening as he put pen to paper at his home in Monticello. By the end of Jefferson's life, evangelical Christianity was more deeply rooted in society than ever before.

Back in 1966, *Time* magazine ran a story, "Toward a Hidden God," exploring the relationship of humans to God in modern society. The magazine cover stating "Is God Dead?" garnered even more attention than the article itself. The article was not exactly as anti-God as the cover implied. Nonetheless, the article did suggest that views of God were shifting in the era of the '60s. In 2009, *Newsweek* ran a story called "The Decline and Fall of Christian America" that brought up some of the same issues of the previous story.[3]

When we look deeper into the current state of faith in America, however, we see a much more complex situation. While Christianity may be in decline in some segments of our society, that decline is not as profound, if at all, in other communities. While not immune to decline, many Black Churches and communities still have a legacy of *unshakable faith*. This is reflected in George Barna's 2020 study of Black Church trends, an update on a 2000 study of the same.

What Scripture and studies do tell us is that diversity is important to the strength of our faith. America's increasing diversity, instead of being a sign of our nation's eroding values, is a base where evangelical faith is thriving. In African American, Latin, and Asian communities, Christianity is finding younger voices. This diversity will not only bring changes to our nation in our desire to be more inclusive ethnically, but it will also bring welcome changes to the church.

When we think about who an evangelical is, the first person that may come to mind is someone from an underrepresented group. Today the media often portrays an evangelical in a very different way, by conflating the term *evangelical* with *white*. In the process, it dismisses the experiences and views of Black, Latino, and Asian evangelicals.

While the low percentage of Christian believers in many Western countries is alarming, a look to the Global East and South should encourage all of us. In China, numerous African nations, the Philippines, and elsewhere, Christianity is thriving. At the same time, in Poland and other formerly communist, post-Soviet nations and Cuba, Christianity is experiencing a period of revival.

It may be easy for some to conclude that religion is in decline; the reality is that our nation's growing ethnic diversity is a tremendous opportunity for spiritual growth. If Christian communities are willing to openly address longstanding issues of racism and ethnocentrism, it could lead to another revival. If we are unable to do so, our numbers may well decline as young people look to other options such as secular humanism.[4]

Signs of Hope

I am an optimist, and I believe that those of us who believe in the good news should be. Our faith is not dead. Jesus is alive and always relevant—as well as necessary—in our society. The opportunity to have the difficult conversations about racism and prejudice is here—and we can be successful.

That some people are leaving the faith does not surprise me. As Christian communities, we have not always been the best advocates of our faith. We often speak about what we *do not* believe in rather than what we *do* believe in. Instead of instilling hope, all too often we are overtly negative. In a society where significant numbers of people suffer from depression, anxiety, drug abuse, and hopelessness, negativity is not going to be a successful strategy to spread the good news.

Jesus gives joy. Psalm 94:19 says, "When anxiety was great within me, your consolation brought me joy." This joy does not mean that everyone who has abandoned their faith ends up depressed, nor does it mean that all believers will be protected from these conditions. What our faith does give us is hope. Without that hope, I believe we would go down the road to nihilism.

Secular humanism and other popular belief systems will never sustain us in the way that Christ redeems and strengthens. When I bow down at night to pray to my Master, there is a calmness that resides within me as I realize my humanity. Only Jesus can do that. From God flows our sense of morality. From His pathways, we look at the world. It was He who documented our value system.

Sadly, numerous studies have revealed that millennials have a surprising lack of empathy compared to previous generations.

Indeed, as a society our ability to connect with others and to feel others' pain has declined.[5] In a society that prioritizes individual desires and lusts over the sanctity and diversity of human life, we need God to fill in our lack of empathy for the most vulnerable in society. All of these conditions provide an opportunity to spread our faith through the power of reconciliation.

At their best, our faith communities provide loving and stable environments. Here we know that God loves us, but we also know that we have a community of accountability partners and others who truly care about what happens to us.

As members of faith communities, it's important that we do not fall victim to the negative patterns we see in our society. Our faith communities should resist the tendency to isolate ourselves. We need to stake out a higher level of connectivity to others. Communities with empathy and compassion transform people's lives, as our history affirms. Our words and witness to those who are struggling may be what invites others to seek Jesus or pushes them away.

I believe that there is tremendous opportunity for revival. I am persuaded that we are starting to see a new revival if we only open our eyes and "press on toward the goal to win the prize for which God has called [us] heavenward in Christ Jesus (Philippians 3:14). While it seems as if polls and the media are fixated on stories of Christians leaving their faith, many people are accepting Jesus and rededicating their lives to Him.

In the entertainment world, there are many examples. Several well-known musicians in the hip-hop world are pursuing Christian faith and appear to be making steps to proclaiming it.

PRESS ON TOWARD THE GOAL TO WIN THE PRIZE FOR WHICH GOD HAS CALLED [US] HEAVENWARD IN CHRIST JESUS. (PHILIPPIANS 3:14)

Chance, Kanye, and Kendrick: Hope and Prayers for the Future

One may think that the entertainment world is totally sinful. Indeed, the hip-hop world is not often highlighted for its piety. However, if we look closely, there are signs of a revival within the industry. While musicians such as well-known Christian hip-hop artist Lecrae have been recognized as such throughout their careers, other artists such as Kendrick Lamar, Chance the Rapper, and Kanye West are not necessarily identified as Christian or gospel artists. Nevertheless, each of them has publicly expressed their Christian faith and their faith has found a place in their music. Even more exciting is that each of these men are young. Chance the Rapper was born in 1993; Kendrick Lamar in 1987; and Kanye West in 1977. Chance the Rapper and Kendrick Lamar are millennials, while West was born at the end of Generation X.

One day we may compare these three men to these other musicians whose faith journeys we've learned about: Duke Ellington, Thomas Dorsey, and Ethel Waters. In no way are any of these three men perfect. None of us are! Some of them continue to use profanity in their music. However, each of them has, at least at some level, begun to show that his path has the potential to follow a similar one to that of young Thomas

Dorsey, whose blues songs remained profane while he was at the same time attempting to jump-start his life as well as a gospel music career.

When I consider Kendrick Lamar, I realize that it is hard on the surface to identify his music as Christian—at this time. Kendrick Lamar was born during the height of the drug wars in in Compton, California. Compton was a community full of drugs and gangs, where murder was commonplace. Lamar was raised in Section 8 housing. His father was a member of the Gangster Disciples, one of the most dangerous gangs in Los Angeles.

These experiences—including being surrounded by drugs, prostitution, and gangs—come up regularly in Lamar's music. When Lamar released his first album, it was little surprise that it included a song like "A.D.H.D." This song, with its continuous references to rampant drug use in his community and the grotesque effects of the drug wars and crack epidemic on Black and brown communities, is not only autobiographical, but it is the story of many young Black and brown people who grew up in 1990s America.

Lamar witnessed the mass incarceration of young Black men. He felt what it was like living in a society where one in three men like him would go to prison sometime during their life. Little wonder why Lamar's perspective is bleak and nihilistic— what else might we expect?

Continuing to develop and use his voice, one year after releasing "A.D.H.D," Lamar released his second album *Good Kid, M.A.A.D. City.* Even more than his previous record, this one explores his religious faith. Indeed, the opening of the album begins with the sinner's prayer. Throughout the album, there are numerous references to Lamar's understanding that he is a sinner in need of the Lord's forgiveness so that he can be saved. In one song in particular, "Sing about Me, I'm Dying of Thirst," Lamar then discusses the death of a friend who was living the gangster lifestyle. Lamar doesn't just recount his friend's death. He explores his belief in the Holy Spirit and his hope that Jesus will wash away his sins.

In Lamar's third studio album, his references to his faith expand to the meaning of temptation and sin. In the song "I," Lamar proclaims that he knows God even though he is tempted and will go through tribulations.

The themes of sin and temptation permeate Kendrick Lamar's music. Throughout his lyrics, he states that only Jesus can help us overcome obstacles. At the same time, as numerous other outlets have noted, Lamar's music speaks to his belief in God's judgment. Lamar wrote in an email to the Hip Hop website DJ Booth:

> Though his son died for our sins, our free will to make whatever choice we want, still allows him to judge us. So, in conclusion, I feel it's my calling to share the joy of God, but with exclamation, more so, the FEAR OF GOD. . . . Knowing the power in what he can build, and also what he can destroy.

Lamar continues, saying that God is "a jealous God," who requires "obedience" and who corrects "every conscious choice of sin" with "his discipline."[6]

Although Kendrick Lamar is experiencing a religious transformation, he at this writing—and he would be the first to admit it—is not where he wants to be, considering the lyrics of his songs. Although his theology is not yet fleshed out, it is encouraging to see this young Black man, in the world that Lamar is speaking to, so blunt and open about Christian faith. He may not express his faith the way that you or I may want or expect from a Christian, but he is also taking the Word to communities in need.

When I was growing up in the 1990s, I even looked at the acknowledgments of artists on their CDs. It made an impact when I saw that they acknowledged their faith. Lamar's testimony has the ability to inspire many young men struggling with their faith.

Lamar also shows us the obstacles we face in our nation. In order to reach people from his generation and community—we need to do a better job of understanding and addressing the consequences of systemic racism and the drug wars. Outside of doing this, it will be difficult to move forward in conversation and collaboration.

If Kendrick Lamar's faith is more focused on God's judgment, Chance the Rapper's faith, even though he is the youngest of the young triumvirate, has developed a more evangelical tone. Raised in a Christian home that was politically active and solidly middle class, Chance the Rapper had a much different life than Kendrick Lamar. His father was involved in politics and worked with others who were, from first Black mayor of Chicago Harold Washington to former president Barack Obama.

As Chance entered high school, his desires turned toward the world and what the world had to offer. By his senior year, he got involved with drugs and was even suspended for using marijuana. During his suspension, he documented these experiences in songs that would eventually be part of his first album *10 Day*.[7] By the time his second album, *Acid Rap*, came out, Chance's drug use had graduated to LSD. Riding a wave of success, Chance left his hometown in Chicago and moved to Los Angeles. After moving there, Chance started using Xanax.[8] The combination of drugs and bad relationships threatened to derail his career and life.

Upset with the direction his life was going, Chance started to reach out to God. In an interview with *GQ* magazine, Chance gave a hint of what began to turn him around. It was his grandmother and spiritual mentor.

> And she looked me in the eyes and she said, "I don't like what's going on." She said, "I can see it in your eyes. I don't like this." And she says, "We're gonna pray." And she prayed for me all the time. Like, very positive things. But this time, she said, "Lord, I pray that all things that are not like You, You take away from Chance. Make sure that he fails at everything that is not like You. Take it away. Turn it into dust."[9]

Listening to his family's encouragement, he started to recommit his life to Christ. Even then, his life did not become perfect. He made the choice to go back to his girlfriend, who is now his wife. Believing that Los Angeles had too many temptations, Chance made an even bigger choice by deciding to leave Los Angeles and move back to Chicago. By 2017, he was clean and no longer taking LSD or Xanax. His experiences getting clean even provided inspiration for his music. He referenced this in his song, "All My Friends." His life wasn't perfect, and he continued to have challenges. He also continued to work on his relationship with his then girlfriend. They had a child born with a congenital heart disorder and were estranged for a time.

During this period, his struggles led him back to the church. He wrote on his Twitter feed: "Today's the last day of my old life, last day smoking cigs. Headed to church for help. All things are possible thru Christ who strengthens me."[10]

Around the same time, Chance began recording his new album *Coloring Book*. In that same year, he provided a verse on Kanye West's song "Ultralight Beam." Ironically, this song was a hint of Kanye West's recommitment to his Christian faith. In this song, Chance and West team up with gospel recording artists Kelly Price and Kirk Franklin. Chance's verse spoke about resilience and the power of forgiveness.

As the song reveals, Chance's music had developed spiritually. He was more contemplative in his music and in exploring his faith. Being healed from the temptation of drug addiction, he credited God for his deliverance. This was a message that Chance wanted the entire world to know.

Chance's transformation continues through *Coloring Book*. From "How Great," which is a remake of "How Great Is Our God," to "All We Got." "How Great" is an ode to God's majesty, while "All We Got" is an exploration of his losses and struggles that brought him to a breaking point, where he recognized that all he had was God's love and Jesus's redemption. *Coloring Book* can be seen as a dedication to his newfound faith: "I never really set out to make anything that could pretend to be new gospel or pretend to be the gospel," he said. "It's just music from me as a Christian man because I think before I was making music as a Christian child. And in both cases I have imperfections, but there was a declaration that can be made through going through all the [stuff] I've been through the last few years."[11]

Who Are We to Judge?

As Christians, we should not rush to judgment. In each of our lives, God's grace is sufficient and He loves us regardless of who we are. Imagine if God judged us the way we judge others. In Dorsey's case, it was church people who helped push him toward depression and, ironically, led him back to secular music.

In 2016, Lecrae, who has been remarkably consistent in his Christian walk, declared his support for Black Lives Matter. Even though Lecrae went to great lengths to say that he agreed with the "sentiment" of the words and not necessarily the organization behind it, the oppositional response from many in the Christian community left him, in his own words, drained.[12]

God through His love shows us a model of community. Community doesn't push aside people just because they express support of an issue they find important. God shows us empathy and compassion. Lecrae's experiences are further proof of a lack of empathy in our society that has entered into the church. If our job is to lift one another up, it is a shame that many Christians refuse to try to empathize with the life of the oppressed. Empathy is key to our Christian walk.

Kanye West is another individual who has experienced a transformation in his life. His album *Jesus Is King* was the number-one album in our nation in October 2019. Although West has proclaimed his faith before in songs such as "Jesus Walks" and the aforementioned "Ultralight Beam," he largely was not defined by his faith. West is widely recognized as one of the greatest rappers of all time. At the same time, West is notorious for participating in numerous antics simply to garner attention.

All of this changed after he had a *born-again* experience. Since then, he has used his musical talents to spread the Word. He has dedicated his life to spreading the Word through his sponsoring of Sunday Service events. Yet even with all the good he is doing spreading the gospel, people sometimes focus on his politics as a way to either support or critique his overall message.

As Christians, it is not our job to question the sincerity of other Christians. When we do this, it actually says more about us and our politics than it does about their faith journeys. Instead of celebrating the open faith of Lecrae, Lamar, and Chance the Rapper, many on the evangelical right either refuse to acknowledge their conversion or criticize their connection to social-justice issues. The same side used to criticize Kanye West as well when he confronted President Bush and his administration's response to Hurricane Katrina. When West adopted a different political philosophy, some on the evangelical left criticized his political alliances, using their own perceptions to make a statement about his faith.

Our faith is a big tent. Jesus hung out with all types of people; some we may call saints, and others we would definitely call sinners. In a society of litmus tests and purity tests, too many of us place too many of these tests on our fellow Christians—litmus tests that go beyond the sinner's prayer. Of course, our faith informs our political and social decisions but all too often we place our own values over the simplicity of Jesus's call.

When we look at each of these men, we should recognize that they are beginning a journey—one that we all should pray they continue to grow in by the grace of Jesus Christ. We should pray for encouragement for them to continue to study and to discern. We should hope and pray for future generations to be inspired by the relevance of Jesus in a complicated modern world. We should pray that God continues to raise up leaders, giving them His Spirit and peace.

The Bible informs us that Jesus hung out with the sinners and tax collectors—people on the margins (Luke 15:2). I know that He helped pick me up when I was at my lowest point. I'm so glad that the people around me didn't ask me questions about who and what I was back then. I wasn't where I needed to be. Yet, God led me to a transformation where I was going to eventually win that race.

When I see reports of a thousand people committing their lives to Christ at Kanye West's Sunday Service, I don't think about whether he is a Democrat or Republican, I celebrate because I know what it means to be saved.[13]

Instead of judging, let's pray for the continuation of their Christian journeys.

REFLECTIONS, PRAYERS FOR HEALING, AND A FINAL DEVOTION

A Devotion of Redemption

> The thief comes only to steal and kill and
> destroy; I have come that they may have life,
> and have it to the full. (JOHN 10:10)

Redemption is the key to our Christian experience. The profiles in this book have all demonstrated the power of being redeemed. Being rescued through the saving work of Jesus does not mean that we do not struggle with sin; yet we are redeemed from it. To be born again means we are cleansed and given power through the Holy Spirit, who guides us from there.

I remember the point in my life when I was in the pit, but Jesus renewed me. When I looked in the mirror, I hated what I saw and what I had become. Jesus came to me and let me know that He loved me just as I was and that His love for me is so great that He sacrificed himself for me. How could I not love myself if God loves me so? How could I not get up, since Christ rose from the dead?

Throughout history, there are many examples of people in difficult situations who found the power to move forward. I will share a final story as we conclude, as another testimony and encouragement toward our unshakable faith.

Former slave Charles Ball, separated from his family, wanted to be reunited with them.

As a slave, he had been chained and taken from his family while asking his master if he could be "allowed to go to see my wife and children." If this could not be permitted, he asked "if they might not have leave to come see me." The master responded that Ball could get another wife once he was in Georgia.[14]

Understanding the legacy of separation in the African American community, as well as our desire to be redeemed with God, family, and our nation, it should not be a surprise that the idea of redemption holds a special place in African American heritage. Redemption has a spiritual meaning in that it means to be redeemed—restored—*to God*. The word *redemption* also means to pay a debt.

Black people throughout American history recognized what it was like to have their life or children stolen from them. Therefore, for Black people, redemption has both spiritual and symbolic meanings. We see the theme of redemption woven through generations of African American literature, in Black cinematic productions—from Spencer Williams, Ava DuVernay, to Tyler Perry—and redemption is preached every Sunday at worship services.

Charles Ball's life exemplifies in so many ways the African American experience and why redemption matters to us. Born a slave in Maryland around 1780, Charles Ball was sold in his early years to South Carolina. Ball desired redemption from bondage. He actually escaped captivity and returned to Maryland. There, he was reunited with his family. He became a free man.

He served his nation during the War of 1812. When the war broke out, Ball enlisted to support his nation, although the British may have provided him his freedom if he had fought on their side. He later married and had a family. Sadly, after serving his nation, he was captured and returned to slavery. We have no historical knowledge that he was ever reunited with his family or saw them again.

As descendants of American slavery and generations of oppression, many African Americans understand Charles Ball's emotions. Throughout history, African Americans have held out hope for the day that their sacrifices for our nation will lead the way toward redemption. Even though African Americans do not owe our nation a debt, they have all too often been forced to pay one.

I believe this is the reason why family reunions are so important in our community. Redemption and reunion hold a special place in our culture as descendants of slaves. Our ancestors may have been sold, just as Charles Ball was. Many African American families passed down stories of degradation and permanent separation from their family members. So many of our ancestors never again saw those who were sold in their presence during their lifetimes, but they hoped and prayed for a day of redemption.

Separated from her homeland and her parents, Phillis Wheatley, along with so many like her, certainly looked toward a day of redemption and reunion.

Historically, African Americans have sought redemption with God, with our nation, and with ourselves. When we read

SEPARATED FROM HER HOMELAND AND HER PARENTS, PHILLIS WHEATLEY, ALONG WITH SO MANY LIKE HER, CERTAINLY LOOKED TOWARD A DAY OF REDEMPTION AND REUNION.

the Declaration of Independence, we do not think about the fact that Thomas Jefferson was a slave owner; we think about the fact that he wrote "all men are created equal." Even though it was not a reality at that point, we hoped and prayed that one day we would be redeemed in our nation and that we would be fully accepted into the American citizenry. W. E. B. Du Bois expressed the pull of our two selves.

> The history of the American Negro is the history of this strife,—this longing to attain self-conscious manhood, to merge his double self into a better and truer self. In this merging he wishes neither of the older selves to be lost. He would not Africanize America, for America has too much to teach the world and Africa. He would not bleach his Negro soul in a flood of white Americanism, for he knows that Negro blood has a message for the world. He simply wishes to make it possible for a man to be both a Negro and an American, without being cursed and spit upon by his fellows, without having the doors of Opportunity closed roughly in his face.[15]

As African Americans, our stories are part of the underpinnings of these United States. To be American and Black. Faith has been the glue that ties our twoness. Unshakable faith has sustained us in this struggle. The faith stories of our ancestors provided the rocks from which our pillars of faith are secured. As a people, African Americans have reso-lutely held to the promise of redemption by relying on Jesus, who has come to us in our dreams, our hopes, our prisons, and our enslavement.

Throughout this journey of our history, we have been joined by others from many different backgrounds. We have never been alone. But it has often been a tough and lonely journey.

It is my hope that these stories not only demonstrate the power of faith in the Black community but also reveal the way that unshakable faith can bring diverse people together. I hope that this inspires more collaboration. I know that our faith can serve as a vehicle to help us press forward and push for redemp-tion across our nation's great divides.

To do so, we must invite the Holy Spirit to guide us to greater wisdom and toward redemption. "That all of them may be one, Father, just as you are in me and I am in you. May they also be in us so that the world may believe that you have sent me" (John 17:21).

Amen.

Explore Your Faith

*   How can more mature Christians be better supporters of young people just coming to the faith and not push them away?

*   What ways do we all need redemption and reunion?

*   What role can we all play to ensure that our fellow Christians do not feel abandoned and lonely, especially those who are different from us?

ACKNOWLEDGMENTS

To my dearest wife, Almie, I am so grateful that God has placed you in my life. Your spirit and love have inspired me to dream and to follow God's direction. You have supported me through the entirety of this book. You have also sacrificed in immeasurable ways. Through all my ups and downs in life, you have been right there praying for and encouraging me. For everything you are—I am eternally grateful.

To my father, Carey III, thank you for always being there. Thank you for teaching me what it means to be a man, father, and leader. Thank you for your actions that have shown me the importance of humility and service. You are the rock that has held our family together. I am thankful to God for the time we have had and continue to share together.

To my mother-in-law, Milagros, thank you for accepting me into your family. Your wisdom and unyielding faith continue to inspire me to reach higher heights.

To my sisters, Kimberly and Kerri, thank you for leading the way as well. It's not always easy being the youngest child in a family. But I have always had both of you to show me the way.

To my Pastor, Otis Mitchell, and my brothers and sisters in the ministry at Mount Zion First Baptist Church in San Antonio, Texas, thank you for your support and love over the last sixteen years. I am truly blessed to belong to a church of strong, faithful believers.

To my family at Antioch Baptist Church in Saluda, Virginia, I thank you, too. It was at this church that I learned the power of faith, where my ancestors, once freed, worshipped. I am so glad that I was able to sit, pray, and sing in that same church for so many years of my life. To Rev. Fred Holmes, thank you for encouraging me from the very beginning to follow God.

To Father Kevin Fausz, thank you, too, for encouraging me in the ministry. You have encouraged me to think deeply on so many points of our great faith.

I also thank my colleagues in the History Department at Trinity University. Even though this project is not a traditional project in our field, I am thankful that you have encouraged me to pursue my dreams.

To the members of my editorial team, including Arthur Jackson, Anna Haggard, and Toria Keyes, thank you for your commentary on this project. I am so thankful for the time you spent reading drafts and providing excellent commentary. Thank you for making the process so enjoyable.

To Joyce Dinkins, words cannot express how blessed I am for your belief in this project. I still remember the conference where we first met and you asking me whether I had a project in my spirit. I did, but I wasn't sure it could end up as a book. You believed in it from the beginning. And you have steered this project, read numerous drafts, and kept the faith throughout.

To my Lord, *thank you*!

NOTES

Chapter 1

1. In using the word *America*, my intent is to convey what we often refer to as *British North America* or what will eventually become the *United States*.

2. Note that the Europeans came to a land already settled by Native Americans. The interactions between Europeans and Africans with the Native Americans are too numerous to explore in this book.

3. John Winthrop, "A Model for Christian Charity," in *The Puritans in America: A Narrative Anthology*, eds. Alan Heimert and Andrew Delbanco (Cambridge, MA: Harvard University Press, 1985), 82–92. Hereafter, listed as Winthrop, "A Model for Christian Charity."

4. Linda Heywood and John Thornton, *Central Africans, Atlantic Creoles, and the Foundation of the Americas, 1585–1660* (New York: Cambridge University Press, 2007), 320.

5. Benjamin Franklin, *The Autobiography of Benjamin Franklin* (United States: P. F. Collier, 1909), 104–108.

6. Franklin, 105.

7. Ira Berlin, *Slaves Without Masters: The Free Negro in the Antebellum South* (New York: New City Press, 1974), 59–61; Andrew Levy, *The First Emancipator: The Forgotten Story of Robert Carter, The Founding Father Who Freed His Slaves* (New York: Random House, 2005).

8. Francis J. Bremer, *John Winthrop: America's Forgotten Founding Father* (Oxford: Oxford University Press, 2005), 173.

9. Winthrop, "A Model for Christian Charity," 91.

10. Melvin H. Buxbaum, "Cyrus Bustill Addresses the Blacks of Philadelphia," *The William and Mary Quarterly* 29, no. 1 (January 1972), 99–104, https://doi.org/10.2307/1921329. Hereafter noted as *Bustill*. Please note that from here I have cleaned up the spelling from Bustill's speech. Both the meaning and content remain the same.

11. Anna Bustill Smith, "The Bustill Family," *The Journal of Negro History* 10, no. 4 (October 1925), 638, https://doi.org/10.2307/2714143.

12. Smith, "Bustill Family," 638; Bustill, 99.

13. Gary B. Nash, *Forging Freedom: The Formation of Philadelphia's Black Community, 1720–1840* (Cambridge: Harvard University Press, 1988), 100–105.

14. Smith, "Bustill Family," 638–644.

15. Nash, *Forging Freedom*, 60–65.

16. Bustill, 104.

17. Bustill, 105.

18. Bustill, 105.

19. Smith, "Bustill Family," 639.

20. Phillis Wheatley, *Poems on Various Subjects, Religious and Moral* (United Kingdom, 1793), 6; Henry Louis Gates and Nellie Y. McKay, *The Norton Anthology of African American Literature* (New York: W.W. Norton & Co., 1997), 164–167.

21. Vincent Carretta, *Phillis Wheatley: Biography of a Genius in Bondage* (Athens: University of Georgia Press, 2014), 7.

22. Caretta, 7.

23. Phillis Wheatley to Obour Tanner, March 21, 1774, https://www.loc.gov/item/rbpe.0370260b/.

24. Gates and McKay, *Norton Anthology of African American Literature*, 164–167.

25. Gates and McKay, 164–167.

26. Phillis Wheatley, "Letter to Reverend Samson Occom," *The Connecticut Gazette*, March 11, 1774.

27. Samson Occom, "A Short Narrative of My Life," typescript, Dartmouth College Archives, in Bernd Peyer, *The Elders Wrote* (Berlin: Dietrich Reimer Verlag, 1982), 12–18.

28. Phillis Wheatley, "On Being Brought from Africa to America," in *Poems on Various Subjects, Religious and Moral*, 15. Throughout the rest of the chapter, individual poems from this work are cited with the author's name.

29. Wheatley, "On Being Brought from Africa to America," 15.

30. Wheatley, "To the Right Honorable William, Earl of Dartmouth," 54.

31. Wheatley, "On the Death of the Rev. George Whitefield," 18.

32. Wheatley, 19.

33. Wheatley, "A Funeral Poem on the Death of C.R., an Infant of Twelve Months," 50.

34. Wheatley, "On the Death of Young Lady of Five Years of Age," 21.

35. Wheatley, 21.

36. Wheatley, "To the Rev. Dr. Thomas Amory on Reading His Sermons on Daily Devotion, in which That Duty Is Recommended AND Assisted," 66.

37. Wheatley, "On the Death of Rev. Dr. Sewell, 1769," 18.

38. Wheatley, "Thoughts on the Works of Providence," 42.

39. Wheatley, "To the University of Cambridge in New England," 13.

Chapter 2

1. George Whitefield, "Marks of a True Conversion" in *Sermons of George Whitefield* (New Haven, 1834), 71.

2. George Whitefield, "The Seed of the Woman, and the Seed of the Serpent in George Whitefield," in *The Works of the Reverend George Whitefield* (Edinburgh, 1771), 16.

3. James P. Eckman, *A Covenant People: Israel from Abraham to the Present* (Bloomington, IN: WestBow Press, 2014), 283.

4. William A. Smith, *Lectures on the Philosophy and Practice of Slavery* (Nashville: Stevenson and Evans, 1956), 277.

5. Henry Highland Garnet, "An Address to the Slaves of the United States of America" (lecture, National Convention of Colored Citizens, Buffalo, New York, August 16, 1843).

6. Nat Turner and Thomas R. Gray, *The Confessions of Nat Turner* (Richmond, 1832), 7, https://www.loc.gov/item/07009643/.

7. Turner and Gray, 9.

8. Paul Cuffe, *A brief account of the settlement and present situation of the colony of Sierra Leone, in Africa* (New York, 1812), 3 and 9, https://www.loc.gov/item/24017195/.

9. Isaac Van Arsdale Brown, *Memoirs of the Rev. Robert Finley, D. D., Late Pastor of the Presbyterian Congregation at Basking Ridge, New-Jersey, and President of Franklin College, Located at Athens, in the State of Georgia. With Brief Sketches of Some of His Contemporaries, and Numerous Notes* (New Brunswick, Canada, 1819), 77.

10. Brown, 90.

11. There is only one race, but the people we discuss in this book believed that races did indeed exist.

12. Brown, *Memoirs*, 91.

13. Abigail Mott, *Biographical Sketches and Interesting Anecdotes of Persons of Color: To which is Added a Selection of Pieces in Poetry* (New York, 1839), 114.

14. Ralph Randolph Gurley, *Life of Jehudi Ashmun, Late Colonial Agent in Liberia: With an Appendix, Containing Extracts from His Journal and Other Writings; with a Brief Sketch of the Life of the Rev. Lott Cary,* 2nd ed. (New York, 1839), 148.

15. Miles Mark Fisher, "Lott Cary the Colonizing Missionary," *The Journal of Negro History* 7 (October 1922), 384.

16. Gurley, *Life of Jehudi Ashmun*, 148.

17. *History of the Missions of the Baptist General Convention*, quoted in Fisher, "Lott Cary the Colonizing Missionary," 387.

18. Gurley, 148.

19. Lott Cary to Dr. Staughton, March 13, 1821, in James Barnett Taylor, *Biography of Elder Lott Cary, Late Missionary to Africa* (Baltimore, 1837), 28.

20. Fisher, "Lott Cary the Colonizing Missionary," 394.

21. Cary Letter in Gurley, *Life of Jehudi Ashmun*, 149–150.

22. Gurley, 149.

23. Lott Cary to William Crane, August 16, 1823, in Taylor, *Biography of Elder Lott Cary*, 42–44.

24. Lott Cary to friends in Virginia, April 24, 1826, in Taylor, 62.

25. Lott Cary to friends in Virginia, April 24, 1826, in Taylor, 62–63.

26. Gurley, *Life of Jehudi Ashmun*, 160.

27. David Walker, *Walker's Appeal, in Four Articles: Together with a Preamble, to the Colored Citizens of the World, But in Particular, and Very Expressly to Those of the United States of America* (Boston, 1830), 14.

28. Walker, 35.

29. Maria W. Stewart, "Lecture Delivered at the Franklin Hall, Boston, September 21, 1832," in Maria W. Stewart, *Meditations from the Pen of Mrs. Maria W. Stewart* (Washington, DC, 1879), 56.

30. Stewart, *Meditations from the Pen*, IV.

31. Stewart, 24.

32. Stewart, 24.

33. Stewart, "Lecture Delivered at the Franklin Hall, Boston, September, 31, 1832," in *Meditations from the Pen*, 55.

34. Stewart, 55.